AF335038

If You Did What I Asked in the First Place

If You Did What I Asked in the First Place

Lori B. Duff

Deeds Publishing | Athens

Printed in The United States of America

Cover design by Mark Babcock. Text layout by Matt King.

ISBN 978-1-947309-70-8

Books are available in quantity for promotional or premium use. For information, email lori@loriduffwrites.com.

First Edition, 2019

10 9 8 7 6 5 4 3 2 1

This book is dedicated to my father, because once not too long ago when my mother and I were playing Scrabble, he tried to help her and put down "Baar." My mother said, "What is that?" and I started singing, "Daveeeeeeeeeey . . . Davey Crockett, king of the wild frontier." My dad sang back, "Killed him a baar when he was only three . . . " And it made me think how nice it is when someone gets your jokes, no matter how obscure or objectively not funny they may be.

Thanks for teaching me how to laugh at my own jokes, Papa, whether or not anyone else laughs with me. And thanks for getting my jokes. That's even better.

And thanks to you, Mom, for still being willing to play Scrabble with me.

Not many people are.

Contents

If You Did What I Asked in the First Place

I'm pretty sure that nine-tenths of all conversations between married women with children that also include a bottle of wine (or, on some nights, a pitcher of margaritas) involve some variation of a sentence that starts with, "And of course, if they'd done what I asked them to do in the first place . . ."

It's not because we're infallible. It's not because every single opinion we've ever had has turned out to be prophetic in hindsight. It's more because of our motives. Totally jumping into stereotype mode here, people who have these conversations tend to be the caretakers in their family. Whether it was foisted on us by gender-conforming roles, or whether it is borne out of a love for these disobedient fools, we really do want the lives of our loved ones to be as successful and problem-free as possible. Also, because we are the ones who have to clean up the messes when they occur, we'd rather not see them made in the first place because it just adds to our burdens.

It's like when you watch one of those stupid videos of someone riding a bicycle up a homemade ramp because they think it will let them sail over a fence and they end up with a face-full of chicken wire. You can see it coming from a mile away. It's frustrating enough to watch it happen to a stranger. When your family is involved, and you are metaphorically yelling, "If you shoot bottle rockets at each other, someone's hair is going to catch on fire," and then BAM, someone's hair catches on fire, you're allowed to be a little miffed that you have to shell out 40 bucks to get the burnt part cut out in a way that looks like you chose that hairstyle on purpose.

I'm just saying.

I Am Wonder Woman

Lately, I've been obsessed with Wonder Woman. This obsession started long before I knew they were making a Wonder Woman movie—I swear it. You can check the dates on my website if you don't believe me. I even got a fake Wonder Woman tattoo and put it on my tricep. (Still not willing to get a real one.) I loved the Wonder Woman TV show when I was a kid, though to be honest I can't remember the plot of a single specific episode. My memories come in flashes, of Diana Prince spinning around and suddenly being Wonder Woman, of the bracelets deflecting bullets, and the wonderful, wonderful golden lasso with which she wrapped up bad guys and made them tell the truth.

I like the idea of Wonder Woman as much as Wonder Woman herself. Maybe even more so. I mean, her clothes are really not practical at all. I live in the deep south, and even here she'd catch a deathly chill. Cover up, dearie. No one needs to see that much cleavage. And to do all the athletics she does, it seems like she'd need a little more support for the girls than anything strapless could provide.

Aside from the fact that I am a Caucasian female with dark hair and light eyes and an hourglass figure, I don't look much like Lynda Carter[1]

---

1. For those of you who don't know, Lynda Carter is the actress who played Wonder Woman in the original 1970's TV series. Gal Gadot plays Wonder Woman in the current movie series. They are both fabulous women in their own right.

at all. Okay, now that I type that, maybe I look exactly like Lynda Carter, even if there are a few more hours in my hourglass than she had, and my eyes are green instead of blue, and my skin is kind of mottled and bumpy and . . . okay, well, I don't look like Lynda Carter at all. But I like the idea of being Wonder Woman. Neither do I look like Gal Gadot, who is just too impossibly perfect and badass to even talk about.

I have an apron that my crafty mother made me several years ago that looks like a headless Wonder Woman. I love it unreasonably. A few years ago I went to a Halloween party as "Wonder Woman after she turned 40 and had a couple of kids." I wore the apron, a bandana in my hair, and topped the whole thing off with a leopard print bathrobe and house shoes.

My obsession makes gift giving easy for me. For my birthday, I got a pair of insulated Wonder Woman travel mugs. For Hanukkah this year, I got the absolute coolest Wonder Woman watch. It looks like a bracelet, but then you push a button and BAM the time magically swirls into being.

I have a Wonder Woman cuff bracelet, Wonder Woman earrings, a Wonder Woman journal, multiple Wonder Woman t-shirts, a Wonder Woman purse and Wonder Woman pens, which I always use to take notes with in Court because you don't just have any lawyer representing you, you have Wonder Woman.

Heck yeah. I am a woman. And I am wonderous.

This is true. Two perfect human beings who make the world a better place simply by existing incubated inside my body. I can run a law firm and a family and still manage to squeeze out times to write these ridiculous books. The fact that I wake up (most) mornings and have the strength to slap on relatively clean clothes and a bit of mascara is a testament to my awesomeness. A lesser woman would have pulled the covers over her head and blocked out all sound.

I shouldn't say a lesser woman. There is nothing lesser about women who suffer from depression or whose burdens outweigh their essential awesomeness. The world is a harsh, nasty place, difficult for the best of us to face. It's not fair that I happen to have a super power that allows me to face it.

I'm not claiming to be the best of us, or even the best of me on many (okay, most) days. I run out of patience, I forget birthdays, I don't always try as hard as I can, and I'm a big-time sinner like all flawed humans. But for all the people who put me down—for the people in 2012 who actually said out loud when I ran for office "I can't vote for a woman;" for every time the men in the room get addressed by their last names, and I get addressed by my first name; for every time I've been the highest ranking person in the room and yet still asked to run make copies or get coffee—for you guys? I am bullet proof—look at my bracelet! I know the truth—check out my golden lasso!

And the truth is, it is wonderful.

So when I was killing time by wandering around the local Wal-Mart while my daughter and her friends went on a search for glitter[2] and I found myself in the pajama section, you can believe me when I say that my heart stopped and the breath rushed from my lungs. There it was. On a rack. In the beams of heavenly sunlight and the source of the angels' chorus. It was a Wonder Woman onesie. In. My. Size.

I put it in the cart, atop the milk and eggs.

I might have squealed out loud.

Eventually, I caught up with my daughter, who was duly horrified when she saw the purchase. I held it up to my body. "Isn't it AMAZING?" I demonstrated the hood, which had Wonder Woman's iconic headband across the front. I fluttered the cape.

She didn't think it was so great. But her friends did, or they pretended to, maybe because I was their ride home.

---

2. Don't ask.

When we got home, I immediately put it on, took a picture of myself and posted it on Facebook. One friend pointed out that, in the picture, it looked like I had a lactation malfunction. I looked at the outfit in the mirror. There were two dark shadowed lines leading crookedly from the chest to about mid-belly. This was, I presumed, a shadow placed there by the designer to create the illusion that one's rib cage unnaturally angled inward towards one's wasp-waist.[3] Also presumably, the designer did not anticipate that someone as old as I was and as saddled with the effects of gravity as I was would wear this thing. Whereas on someone younger and perkier the shadows would begin mid-rib cage, on someone middle aged they began mid-mammary gland.

Still, I loved it, oddly placed shadows or no.

I wasn't done for the night. I had to wait until midnight to drive to the high school to pick up my son, who would be coming home from his

3. This is a thing that no one's waist actually does, except Lynda Carter's. And we all know she is Wonder Woman for real. (Sorry, Gal.)

marching band performance at the football game. On Facebook, I begged someone to dare me to pick the poor boy up dressed as I was. I got a lot of takers.

And so I did. Being devoid of shame, I could stay in my warm, snuggly, fleecy onesie and drive to the high school in fluff lined fake Crocs. Frankly, I'm not sure why anyone has kids if they aren't going to try to embarrass them. I can't think of anything more fun. Just to up the ante, I took a picture of myself in the onesie, hood up, in the car, in front of the high school, and Snapchatted the picture to my son and all his friends that I knew were on the marching band bus. I sat back in the car, played a few games of Candy Crush, and waited.

Finally, the bus pulled up. It parked just in front of my car, and I sat there, feeling a little silly wearing such stupid clothes. Perhaps this was a bad idea after all.I pulled the hood off my head.

I saw my son bop off the bus and look around. He saw my car and came up to my window. I braced myself for the tirade. Instead, he said, "Mom. Get out of the car. Ms. Frazer wants to see your outfit." I opened the car door and hopped out. Feeling like an idiot, I clung to the car door for support, cursing myself for not having the brass ovaries to stand there in the open parking lot with my legs shoulder width apart and my hands on my hips, striking an Amazonian pose.

Eventually, we all got in the car and headed home. "You weren't embarrassed?" I said.

"No," said Jacob. "I thought it was hilarious. Ms. Frazer loved it."

I was torn. On the one hand, I was proud that I'd raised a self-confident boy who knew funny was funny and shame just gets in the way of a good time. On the other, I was going to have to try harder now to embarrass him. I might just be tapped out of ideas.

No, Wonder Woman hasn't been defeated yet. I'm not going to give up this easily. Wonder Woman ALWAYS wins.

Tweenage Drama Island

Some other Moms of pubescent girls and I have been talking, and we think we've found a solution to our problems that will not only make our lives easier, but possibly make us a metric ton of money.

I'm talking about a reality show, Tweenage Drama Island: Where EVERYTHING Is Personal.

Imagine this: twenty-five 12-year old girls are placed in a remote luxury hotel. They are each given one set of sheets, a bath towel, a hand towel, and a washcloth. Unlimited numbers of tiny shampoo bottles and cleaning supplies, etc. are available to them, but they are all in a supply closet in the basement. A full chef's kitchen is available to them, as well as a supply of fresh meat and vegetables and ingredients like flour and spices. No pre-prepared food is available. There are no boxes of Kraft Mac and Cheese. There is no Ramen, and no Toaster Strudels. There are no maids or landscapers or chefs or anyone grownup to help them out.

Better yet, no Wi-Fi. There is only one computer running Windows XP and they have to take turns.

Aside from strategically placed cameras to film the goings on and to make sure that any cries of "I'm literally dying!" are purely dramatic, they are left on their own for six weeks. Six weeks will ensure that every last one of them, at one point, suffers from life-threatening, debilitating, worse-than-anything-ever-in-the-history-of-always cramps.

I mean, wouldn't you love to see a 12-year old holding a potato in one hand, a brick of cheddar in the other, and staring at a gutted chicken wondering how on Earth she's going to make all of this into nuggets and cheese fries?

Or what happens when there is a wad of hair at the bottom of the pool and no one will own up to it? For that matter, who will bother checking the pool pump and emptying it out and regulating the chemicals?

What will happen if someone stops up a toilet?

You, watching at home, get to drink some of your favorite beverage every time someone says "literally" when they mean "figuratively." You will drink a lot.

Here's my prediction: there'll be one girl who turns into the mother of the group, doing her best to cook edible food and getting her feelings severely out of whack when some other girl says, "you made the mess in the kitchen, you should clean it up" and another girl says, "ew" when she sees that the broccoli touches the otherwise edible (if a little chewy) rice on the plate.

There'll be another girl who immediately assesses that all the other girls are morons. She will find a way to get the morons to do her bidding.

Another girl will be perfectly silent until week five, when she finally completely loses it and writes something obscene on a rival's bathroom mirror with lip gloss. If she's feeling especially feisty, she'll use the Queen Bee's bathroom and refuse to flush. There will be a Queen Bee. There is always a Queen Bee. And the thing is, despite the fact that everyone recognizes her as the most popular and the ruler of the hive, no one actually likes her. It's a weird fact of life.

For the first three weeks, everyone will braid everyone else's hair and compliment the length of everyone else's eyelashes and the wings on their eyeliner, no matter what they actually think or say behind closed doors. For the second three weeks, everyone's hair will be in a bun to hide the fact that they can no longer find their hairbrushes. Their eyelashes will have fallen out due to nutritional issues: they have resorted to eating spoonfuls of flour and pats of butter on the theory that "it's the same ingredients as pancakes."

I don't know. Maybe my friends and I are projecting our daughters' collective lack of survival skills on everyone else's. But I'd still watch that show. And I'd love how grateful our daughters would be when they came back to an environment in which Mommy is always there to help pick up the pieces.

And maybe we Mommies would learn that picking up the pieces all the time is what created this problem in the first place.

The Whine of the Motorcycle Rider

There are two kinds of people in this world: People who think adrenaline is fun and exciting and a fresh breath of life, and people who think adrenaline is the stuff of anxiety and ulcers. Me, I'm of the ulcer variety. My husband, the former police helicopter pilot? Yeah, he's a junkie.

As a result, we differ greatly on the subject of motorcycles. I don't see the appeal. When I see a motorcycle, I think of broken femurs and peeled off skin. I hear ambulance sirens and shrieks of pain. Mike thinks of freedom and flying and hears in his head, "VROOOOOOOOOOOOMMMMMMMMMM!"

He wants a motorcycle. I don't want him to have one. I pay his life insurance bill every year just in case he gets one. They're impractical things, I say. They're gas-efficient transportation, yeah, maybe, only without a place to put my purse and a much higher chance to get bugs in my teeth.

Then came Thanksgiving a few years ago. We went to Mike's sister's house. She and her husband were motorcycle-sitting for a friend, and there was a rather impressive looking Harley Davison sitting in the garage. Mike spent a while looking at it, giving me long, drawn out reasons why he would prefer a "crotch rocket" to a Harley. There were lots of sound effects. Harleys, apparently, are muscle machines designed to make you aware of their presence. They go "blumblumblumblum." The sleeker, more need-for-speed models have a higher, whinier, "neeeeeoooooooooooowwwwwwwwwwwwwww," complete with Doppler effect.

But, as they say, beggars can't be choosers, and here was a Harley to ride, not a crotch rocket. To make it 'better' (this word is seriously debatable) we were in South Carolina. The laws of physics had not yet been passed in South Carolina, and so helmets were optional. Mike bounced up and down on the balls of his feet, clapping his hands like a kid on Christmas, absolutely sure his Red Ryder BB Gun was going to be under the tree and could not possibly shoot out an eye. "I've always wanted to ride without a helmet!"

I thought I said, "I've always wanted a husband who didn't have traumatic brain injury." Apparently between the time that the words left my mouth and the time that they reached his ear, the South Carolinian air had twisted them to, "Go right ahead, honey, and be sure to try to break the sound barrier!" And he was off.

He came back, exhilarated and miraculously intact.

He loves me, I think, and so wanted me to feel as pumped up as he was. He begged me to get on the back of the motorcycle with him.

Here's the thing. I am now and was then over 40. There were certain things I had never done in my life, and never felt the need to do. I've never smoked a cigarette. I've never done illegal drugs, not even the more socially acceptable ones like marijuana. (If you are thinking this means I was an uptight, boring teenager, well, then, facts are facts.) It has become a matter of pride for me, now. I'm tempted from time to time, more out of curiosity than anything else, like the time at the Georgia Bar Meeting where they had guys actually rolling cigars at long tables and then handing them out. But, I figure, I've gone this long, why start now. What if I like it?

Well, what if I like it? What if?

And so, because of, or despite the several glasses of pinot grigio I had to accompany Thanksgiving Dinner, I agreed, but only if I could wear a helmet. A search was on, and finally one was scrounged up. It looked like a WWII relic, like maybe the Nazi iron cross had snapped off the top. It felt spongy and weak, like it was more likely to crack and stab me in the head than protect me in case of a crash. But I clung to it like a buoy in the middle of the ocean, believing it would keep me safe from the predatory road.

We went downstairs and got on the motorcycle, my arms circling my husband's belly. There was so much to think about. Which way to lean? How do I make sure that my legs stay away from all the hot pipes? What happens if we run over a stick in the road? Like a bicycle, will it send us tumbling into a ditch?

I insisted we go slowly, and we did. Although it felt like a million miles an hour, I know it was probably more like 25 or 30. I didn't know where to look. Straight ahead was a view of my husband's t-shirt, billowing in the wind. To the side were trees and houses, all going by so quickly. I looked down. The speckles in the asphalt were flowing by, just inches from my feet. I had visions of my foot slipping off the bar it rested on, and being torn off by the road. Each rough pebble of asphalt scraped off my skin in my imagination as I was dragged along by momentum. Road rash, I've heard it called, minimizing it into something that diaper cream could cure in a day or so instead of being flayed by the friction of the road and having my innards exposed like a burn victim.

I think I made it all the way around the block before I made Mike stop and let me get off.

I get why people like it. I do. I really do. I've been on the Jet Ski at the lake, feeling the sun on my face and the wind in my hair, flying across the smooth water, feeling nothing but freedom and joy. I would imagine that's what motorcycle aficionados feel. But I'm not scared of water. I've rolled the Jet Ski a time or two taking a turn too tightly over a wave, and the end result was I got wet, and maybe got a little water up my nose. I didn't eat the back of a tractor trailer or get thrown off into traffic. I didn't even skin my knee. The water is a safety net for me in the way that a crappy, old-school helmet is not.

I'm a cheap date, I guess. Just like I only need one or two glasses of wine to make me completely relaxed and happy, I only need a tiny dose of adrenaline to feel excited.

But I pay my own life insurance premiums, just in case.

A Mother's Lament

Twinkle twinkle little star
Get this trash out of my car
The Taco Bell
The Coffee Cup
Balloons that you were blowing up

Up above the world so high
Somewhere there's a bright blue sky
It can't be seen
Through this dim glass
Through fingerprints and dust and ash

How I wonder what you are
Thinking when you leave this bar
Of chocolate
And nuts galore
A-melting on the backseat floor

Like a diamond in the sky
What's that? Oh, it looks like pie,
A sock, a brush,
A pair of cleats

All smashed into the leather seats

Twinkle twinkle little star
How I wonder what you are
My child, my babe
Born of my flesh
Heart of my hearts: an awful mess.

Out Of My Element

Generally speaking, I feel out of my element so often, I'm not even sure I have an element. I am rough around the edges. I am physically awkward. I say the wrong thing nearly every time I open my mouth. I spill every beverage I've attempted to lift to my mouth, and banged a shoulder against every doorway I've tried to enter.

I'm a New York Jew living in a small southern town. I'm a woman in a traditionally man's profession. I'm a lithe, ballet dancer in a third-string linebacker's body. I'm a loud, opinionated woman who unapologetically doesn't know her place. I mean, literally, I don't know my place. I don't even know where I'm supposed to stand in any given room. It feels like no matter where I stand I'm in someone's way.

But, as I tell myself all the time, "Own the awkward." So here I am, in all my awkward, socially-inept, and overweight glory. Love me or don't. Tolerate my presence or go away. I can't control you and, obviously, I can't control myself, either. I'm working on the serenity to accept that.

Small Talk

My dad, who, left to his own devices, which he never is, would go days without speaking, and who has never once in his life engaged in small talk, will occasionally say this: "When you're born, you're only allowed so many words. If you use them up too soon, you won't be able to speak when you're older." I remember thinking about this as a small child, picturing my voice box as an actual box filled with liquid that dissolved slowly each time I spoke a word. I remember wondering how to ration it properly so as to still be able to say what I wanted but not have to spend my older years as a mute. I wondered how come all the old people I knew were still talking. Surely at least one of them would have run out of words. And did the words "a" or "the" count as much as "antidisestablishmentarianism" or "pneumococcal"? I didn't know who to ask, because it is difficult to tell if my dad, whose poker face is so good he actually hit the money in the World Series of Poker Super Senior tournament last year, is kidding. Also, he would make merciless fun of people who didn't get his jokes, so I didn't want to risk it.

Now that I'm a grownup, I know that he is usually kidding. However, he still repeats that sentiment from time to time, when people go on and on without a particular point. This happens depressingly often.

I don't know if it is because I grew up thinking about using up the words in my voice box, or because I'm just inherently stingy with out-loud words like my dad, but mindless chatter is one of my least favorite things. This is why I'm awful at parties where I'm required to meet people. I've inherited my dad's complete inability to engage in small talk. Small talk is just so... small. I have absolutely no idea what to say that won't sound to my ears like complete drivel. Not that every conversation has to be substantial and thought provoking, but it ought to at least be more interesting than the stray thoughts in my head. And, since I feel like I should treat people the way I want to be treated, I don't pelt their ears with words I don't care about. And therefore, I have exactly zero ability to work a room.

Buddha said, "Don't speak unless it improves the silence." Which is a much less snarky way of making the same point my dad did. Speech is for conveying and discovering information, for making people laugh, for soothing them, and for making sure our needs are met. The way we speak to each other and what we say allows other people to know we care about them. It serves great purpose, and some of my favorite memories involve conversations with interesting people. I'm not anti-speech. I'm not saying that people should only talk in matters of vital importance. I'm just saying that people should do a little inner test to see if what they are saying makes the silence better.

Silence isn't actually something that exists, anyway. For instance, as I write this, I am sitting in a pleather armchair in what is probably referred to by employees as the "bored husband area" of the Mall of Georgia while a bunch of teenagers I drove here shop at Hot Topic for shirts with pithy sayings and pictures of depressing emo bands. I haven't said a word in at least a half hour, and no one has said a word to me. But there is the e-z listening music soundtrack playing; the snippets of conversations as people walk by; the squeak of rubber soled shoes; toddlers having tantrums as they are told they are not going into Build-a-Bear, not today; the rattling of shopping bags; and a host of other ambient noises. I have a decibel meter on my phone, and it says, as I sit here in 'silence,' that I am enjoying the level of noise generally reserved for "normal conversation." (Once, my husband was on the phone with his sister, and he kept getting louder and louder though, to be honest, the conversation was rather boring and not heated at all. I turned the decibel meter on. It said he was at "power tools." We still tease him about that.)

I don't know why our culture doesn't value silence. Companionable silence is one of the best things out there. When you know someone well enough to not feel the societal pressure of yipyap and can just enjoy their presence and the knowledge that if you do want to kick around an idea, they are there to do it: that's the pinnacle of friendship. But no. Normally, it's almost like silence is a vacuum that begs to be filled. We turn on radios and televisions just for background noise. Nature abhors a vacuum; Americans abhor quiet.

Not me, man. Quiet is the BOMB. (A quiet, noiseless bomb that spreads peaceful, fluffy shrapnel over the landscape.)

Huh. That doesn't look right, now that I type it. Maybe I should talk to someone about that.

Erma-Induced Social Anxiety

I am stupidly excited about going to Dayton, Ohio, at the end of this month, even if it has triggered the worst and most irrational of my social anxiety.

I am attending the *Erma Bombeck Writer's Workshop*. This is the kind of workshop that sells out in a few hours. I feel fortunate to be attending, though luck had nothing to do with it: I obsessively refreshed the website starting a few minutes before sign up time so I could get in under the wire. I WORKED for my spot.

And I've been obsessed ever since. I mean, these are my PEOPLE. Or at least the people I want to be considered a part of. Strong, independent, funny women, writing true stories about strong, independent, funny women. I know from the Facebook groups that these are hilarious people: people who have already called me an "ErmaVirgin" and promised me I will make a thousand friends. I'm pretty comfortable with my ability to make friends when I'm communicating in writing.

But what if they don't like me when they look at my face and hear my voice? Generally speaking, I don't give a rip if someone likes me. But these are the people I want to be. There's a number of names of people I've heard of, and some I've admired for some time.

I haven't been this insecure since somewhere around tenth grade. All the social anxiety I thought I'd overcome has come spilling out in waves that might drown me.

Being a detail girl as a general rule, my brain has decided to focus on the stupid details that don't matter. My current obsession is whether or not to get a manicure prior to the Workshop. On the one hand, a manicure will make me feel more 'put together' and confident. On the other, it might make everyone else think that I'm the kind of person who walks around with evenly-sized nails and smooth cuticles on a regular basis. I do NOT want to give a false impression. On the OTHER hand, however, if I go with my regular raggedy nails, will everyone think I'm sloppy in general? And what if I am? Shouldn't they love me for who I am and my sense of humor, rather than whether or not I can find an hour to go get a decent coat of polish on my nails? But what if they DON'T love me for who I am and my sense of humor? What if I turn out to be that loud, obnoxious person with a fake manicure (or nasty scullery-maid hands, depending upon my ultimate decision) who just THINKS she's funny?

To heck with it. I'm funnier when I'm comfortable. I'll just wear yoga pants, college t-shirts advertising events that happened in the late 80s, and no make-up, just DARING everyone to judge me on something superficial.

No, I won't. I wouldn't. I'd want to, but I can't.

Crap. I need to go shopping. What's the weather like in Dayton in late March/early April anyway?

I mean, I know good and well that it is only my anxious ego that is going to be paying attention to my nail beds. There are going to be 300 some-odd women (and a smattering of brave, brave men) who are too busy with their own particularized social anxiety to have the time to pay the least bit of attention to me. I shouldn't flatter myself by thinking that anyone will give me the time of day long enough to give a flippity-flap about my hangnails.

Instead, I should worry about whether anyone will give me the time of day long enough to teach me something about writing, or to make sure I don't have to sit at the lunch table by myself. Or, better yet, worry about whether my own social anxiety will prevent me from making friends with that other woman who has no idea what to wear and is picking at her own cuticles, trying to summon up the courage to go up to someone and say, "Hi."

Home Sweet Hotel Room

As I sit here typing, I am in a hotel room. I'm someone who doesn't generally travel much, but I have been living out of a lot of suitcases lately.

It's not that I'm opposed to travel. The idea appeals to me greatly. There are a lot of places in the world I'd like to go. Unfortunately, all my travel time (and budget) gets spent visiting my out of town parents, attending work-related seminars and conferences, and chaperoning band trips. It's only the 5th weekend of 2017, and I'm chaperoning my second band trip of the year. Long before spring comes, that number will be up to four.

Probably because of a lack of experience, I'm not a very good traveler. I don't ever pack the right clothes. I usually forget something important. I'm forever losing my keys and my wallet, because they don't get put in the place I usually put them, because that place does not exist in a hotel room. It's hard to be a creature of habit in an unfamiliar place.

Hotel rooms themselves creep me out a little. I have to force myself not to think about the dozens of people before me who have breathed and drooled into the same pillow and dried themselves with the same towels. The mattress, even if comfortable, is just different, as are all the ambient sounds like elevator noises, which makes it hard to sleep

Remember being a kid? Whoever you are, wherever you grew up, I'm sure you played some variation on the game "lava." You can only step on the white tiles—the black ones are lava. You can only cross the living room by hopping from couch to chair to table. If you touch the floor, you get burned up in the lava.

Hotel carpeting is all lava. The only thing that can save me from doom is a pair of flip flops (unless I forget them.) I have to hop from the flip flops into the bed, and manage to put on my socks and shoes without my feet ever touching the floor. The flip flops have to be positioned right outside the shower so I don't have to touch the same tile hundreds of bare feet before mine have touched.

I get that much of this is completely irrational. If you've so much as driven by my house, you know I'm not a neat freak or a germophobe under normal circumstances. It has been a long time since I've stayed in a hotel that wasn't at least three stars. I am blessedly well employed enough not to have to stay in suspect hotels. The blindingly white sheets and towels where I stay always smell vaguely of bleach—a clean and reassuring smell. There is nothing rational to fear.

Fear is a strong word, and probably the wrong one. It's more that I feel off-kilter. My stuff isn't where it is supposed to be. I'm not afraid of cooties, and I know I'm unlikely to get anything that can't be cured with an antifungal crème or penicillin. I just prefer the cooties and funk to be my own, I guess.

I'm going back to my cootie infested and funk filled home tomorrow. It will be nice to be back in my own bed where all the pillow drool is my own, but it will still take a couple of days before everything gets back to its rightful place and I can find my keys with regularity. Until Friday, that is, when I chaperone another band trip and pack my suitcase yet again.

With all this practice, you'd think I'd be good at it.

Afternoon Football Fan

I had the opportunity to go to the Chik-Fil-A/Peach Bowl last week. A friend of mine got tickets from a friend of hers, who got them from her husband, who got them from his company. Since they were corporate seats, they were pretty stinking good, right behind the goal post, only 17 rows back. We also got to go to the pregame festivities.I'm not a huge football fan and, in fact, I had no idea who was playing up until the time that my friend June asked me if I wanted to go. (It was Florida State and Houston.) There were extra tickets, so I called my friend Candi, who happens to be as insane a Florida State fan as I am a Duke fan, although probably more, since she actually knows the names of the football players, and I only really care about basketball. Since I believe that sports are only fun if you care who wins, I decided to care about Florida State, since Candi did and we'd be sitting next to each other. I wore garnet-colored pants and a black t-shirt and a gold scarf so I'd look the part.

The pregame festivities were fun. Since we didn't really care about the players much, while everyone else was watching them parade in and trying to get a good luck high five, June's daughter Sydney and I prowled the vendor booths to get free swag while there was no line. Syd, who was there more or less by protest, made a sign at the Home Depot booth which ended up getting her more attention than she bargained for. Turned out a lot of people were also fans of the marching band but never thought to express it. Sadly, her sign didn't get us on the JumboTron or TV.

There was all kinds of great stuff to get. Signs, foam footballs, beef jerky, towels, samples of frozen lemonade, green screen pictures, personalized Chik-Fil-A cows (*man* those Chik-Fil-A people are marketing geniuses),and double insulated cups, just to name a few. Some were up for grabs, some you had to sign up for. Truthfully, I didn't need (or, in retrospect, want) any of it, but I got swept up in the grab. In a weird way, I had a sudden understanding of what made people join in looting. I had this overwhelming urge to take everything I could. Not that I was stealing. People wanted me to take their branded and logo-ed stuff.

At the AT&T booth, they were giving away phone chargers. Phone chargers are at a premium in my house. They get lost as often as socks in the dryer and broken as often as a politician's promises. To get one, you had to post a video on any kind of social media with the hashtag #PeachBowlATT. Since I had no video at my immediate disposal, I quickly filmed one and posted it, and collected my gen-you-wine AT&T phone charger. I have since looked at the video, and realized that a sane (and sober) person would not do such a thing for a $10.00 charger. So I took it down. No. You can't see it.

Of course, not everyone there was stone cold sober at 9:15 a.m. I was truly surprised by the line at the beer carts.

The game was fun, though the 'Noles, who I loved passionately for an entire afternoon, lost. Behind us were the two most rabid Houston

Cougar fans imaginable, one of whom had one of those great big booming baritone voices. He was entirely tone deaf, but sang the fight song every time the pep band played it. He spoke to the players like they could hear him and as if without his encouragement they might give up. "Yes SIR, yes SIR, that's what you need to be doing, we'll give him that one." When he couldn't think of anything else, but there was too much fan-fueled energy to remain silent he yelled something that sounded like "coooooooDOOOWWWW!" It wasn't until the third quarter that I figured out it was "Coug's House!"

All in all, it was a fun game. I paid $5 for some stale popcorn, $10 for a 'personal pan pizza' the size of a dessert plate, and $4 for bottled tap water. And yeah, even the bands were awesome. I was proud to be sitting with their biggest fan.

Hair Helmet

I am in pitiful need of a haircut. My pin straight hair is too heavy and greasy to have any volume in these dry winter days, and so it clings desperately to my skull and the sides of my face in an effort to make my cheeks look as wide as humanly possible. Sometimes one chunk of it will defy gravity, and there'll be some weird lump in it, as if a small woodland creature has created a nest just behind my ear in which to keep its babies warm. No amount of brushing or gel or hairspray can make it move out.

There isn't any real reason why I haven't had a haircut in the past several months, beyond, to use a phrase my children would sink into the carpet with shame if they knew I was using, "Ain't nobody got time for that."

I'm truly amazed by people whose hair is always coiffed and whose nails are always manicured. Even people who manage to swipe on mascara on a weekend are miracle workers in my book. This isn't something I can pull off with any kind of regularity or success.

It isn't that I don't like getting my hair cut or my nails done. I enjoy being pampered, and I always tip the folks who have to deal with my hangnails and scalp-moles well because not only don't I want their jobs, but I recognize how difficult their jobs are and they should be paid well for the convenience of me not having to do it myself. The hairstylist I currently use gives such thorough and satisfactory head rubs while washing my hair that I often feel like lighting up a cigarette when it is over.

So why don't I just go? It isn't an economic thing, like it was when I was a poor student with no income and increasing student loans. I went several years without getting a haircut then. Even a year after I could afford them again, I didn't get them, simply because I got out of the habit. I had extremely long hair, down to my waist. This is something my children marvel at since they have only known me with short hair. I could get away with it then. I was in my early twenties, as fit as I'd ever been or will be, and the world was mine for the taking. Now I'm a Grownup with an Important and Sensible Job, and I do have to look the part for credibility's sake. When my hair is cut, I can blow dry it and hairspray it in less than ten minutes into a style probably listed in the cosmetology school books as "Middle Aged Middle Class Employed Woman." I can still blow dry it and hairspray it in less than ten minutes when it needs to be cut, but the results vary from "meh" to "A+ on the final exams at Clown College."

I don't go to get my hair cut because I can't find the time, which probably means because I can't make the time. Can't or won't, I'm not sure. In order for me to get my hair cut, I need an hour and a half that is unscheduled, where no one needs me to be anywhere else, where I can be out of contact with anyone that doesn't happen to be in the salon and—this is the critical point right here—there isn't something to get done that isn't so pressing that I will undo all the magic of the head rub by tensing my scalp as I think of the papers on my desk that reproduce like over-sexualized bunnies.

All of which means, I suppose, that doing things that have no benefit for anyone outside the confines of my personal self, get prioritized lower than anything else. I think this is a common problem, especially with women with jobs and children. We get so used to Taking Care of Business that we forget that we ourselves are part of the Business We Need to Take Care of. Proof that I am not alone are the scads of articles, in print and online, advising that you have to take care of yourself before you are of use to anyone else. Put the oxygen mask on yourself before assisting other passengers. Alas, no one takes care of the caretaker unless paid to do so. So pony up the cash, girls.

Which is true, in theory, and in many instances, but I'm not sure I buy that entirely. The length or attractiveness of my hair is irrelevant to my mothering or writing or lawyering skills. The raggedness of my cuticles and the lack of polish on my nails doesn't affect my ability to meet a deadline or chaperone every single middle school band festival since time immemorial in an effort to get to know my children's friends and be involved.

No, why it matters is this: to quote Billy Crystal on *Saturday Night Live* in the '80s, to look good is to feel good. When your son's friends point their camera screens at you in order to take a picture for Snapchat, and your first thought is, "Woof!" and not, "How honored I am that teenage girls are willing to give me the time of day and even feature me on their Snapchat stories" you know something is wrong. I don't, generally, care what I look like, or what other people look like, but I do look with pity upon people who just look tired and ragged and unkempt. Just like I believe you have to dress the part at work, you have to look the part of whatever you are playing, or being, or trying to be. Looking your best gives you confidence. A good haircut and a coat of polish on your nails is like a suit of armor to protect you from the insecurity that can ruin a good day.

My kids seem to have figured this out. They both spend more time on their hair than I ever have. My hall bathroom looks like someone tasted the rainbow and it didn't agree with them. Pink, blue, green, bleach, and black stains have seeped into the marble and tile and long outlasted the hair for which the colors were originally intended.

Both of my children, the boychild and the girlchild, have decided that the color of hair growing out of their heads, a color best described as "used coffee grounds" or maybe "topsoil," a color which has served me well for the past 45 years, will not get them out of middle school with their popularity intact.

My daughter started in fourth grade, when I was declared the ONLY mother who did not allow her daughter to have a streak of pink in her hair. I fought it for a short minute, eventually landing on, "it's just hair, and the worst thing that happens is a pixie cut." And the beat went on, in multiple vibrant shades. To paraphrase Crystal Gayle, "And Don't It Make My White Grout Bluuuuuuuuuuuuuue."

My son, being your basic dude, didn't color anything until recently, when he decided he'd try on 'emo' as a personality[4]. He dyed his hair jet black. His sunny personality quickly faded the black, however, so he added blue, which only showed up when the sun shined on him directly. Then he figured he'd bleach all that out and go, as he called it, "Draco Malfoy blonde." This resulted in a faded pinkish color he called, "raw chicken." He hid under a blanket for 18 hours until I got home with dye called, plainly, "brown." He then looked more or less exactly like he did $40 worth of drug store dye ago.

My daughter recently spent her allowance on an intense green dye chosen mainly because of the cuteness of the boy modeling the color on the box. She bleached her purple out to prep, and now has a mass of hot pink curls with white blonde patches, and the occasional natural brown spot sticking out defiantly. Her hair is fried and dry and crinkles when you touch it. I think she looks like someone off-kilter by a mile: someone Helena Bonham Carter would portray in a movie. She thinks she looks awesome.

Eventually my son decided he'd try again, only he saved his money

4. Emo, for those of you who don't deal with teenagers on a regular basis, is short for 'emotional' and is used to describe a subset of teenagers who have sunk entirely into the angsty teenage persona. They wear black skinny jeans and black shirts and paint their nails black, but they aren't to be confused with the 'goth' kids.

and let a professional bleach it and then dye it Cookie Monster blue. The blue is fun, and between that and his height, I can spot him instantly in any crowd.

How did I get from "over my dead body" to "please just dye it a consistent green?" It's a safe rebellion, I suppose, supported by straight A's and nary a detention between them.

Joke's on them, though. Thirty years from now, their kids will see these pictures. I know. I was their age in the '80s.

Battle Scars

Not too long ago, I was hauling some accumulated crapola from one location to another. I hired a U-Haul and several teenagers to help me. We got a late start, and so I was trying to get things moving a little more quickly. Proving the "haste makes waste" adage, in my haste, I made waste to my right shin by walking smack into the trailer hitch on the back of the truck.

It hurt. A lot. I didn't look down right away, for fear that I would see blood streaming down my leg, and maybe a bone shard sticking out, and I didn't have time to tend to any wounds. I did this once before when, back before Craig's List or even before workable internet, I tried to sell my car. A guy came out to look at it. I tripped going up the steps (yes, up) and pulverized my shin. I didn't look because I was too embarrassed. I just carried on like nothing had happened. After he left, I saw a bucket of blood had dripped down and soaked into my socks. That might be why he didn't buy the car.

As it turned out, this time I did not break the skin, but now, almost a week later, I still have an ugly purple bruise the size of my fist that throbs a little every time I take a step. It's lumpy, and it looks gross, and can be seen by anyone looking, possibly from outer space, it is so large and obvious.

It called to mind a rather vivid memory I have of being eight or nine years old. I was standing on the sidewalk and staring down at my legs beneath my skirt, cursing my scabby knees and wondering if there would ever come a time when I could go long enough without falling down and therefore having scabs on my knees. I could never be glamorous or beautiful with scabby knees breaking up the line of my leg.

And here we are, nearly four decades later. My knees aren't scabbed over, but there is the matter of that bruise the size of a small planet. There's also the two-inch line on my left foot left over from bunion surgery, and the three-inch scar on my left arm from when I had to have my wrist held together with an array of metal plates, screws, and pegs. I have a constellation of small scars on my belly from when my gall bladder had to be removed one super fun Christmas Eve.

I have a small, nubbly scar on the inside of my right wrist which came from my early childhood when, twirling around the brass poles that held up velvet ropes in the bank, I twirled directly into my mother's lit cigarette.

There's a half moon scar on my index finger. I got it when I was scraping the caulking out of my bathtub, and the knife slipped and sliced into me.

There's a hairline scar on my thumb that came from cutting bagels the wrong way. (Cut bagels AWAY from your hand—I know this now.)

It's stunning that I don't have more bruises on the outsides of my arms and shoulders, given the number of times I bang into a doorframe, having misjudged the breadth of my upper body.

The takeaway from this is that no matter what I do, I will never have airbrushed model's legs. The lines of my body will always be broken up by scars and bruises and preventable boo-boos. This is because I'm a klutz who considers it a successful day when I don't have to locate a Band-Aid. But also because I'm a person, and these scars are battle scars from a life actually lived.

So, nine-year-old me, the answer is "No." You will never be able to look down at your legs and not see evidence of falling down. But that's okay. Because if you don't fall down, it means you never tried to stand up and do anything.

Middle School Bathroom Ballet

Sometime in late October, I fell out of my car. I have a thousand excuses, none of them particularly good, including "there was stuff in my hands so I couldn't use my arms to balance" and "I parked on uneven turf, making the way out unpredictable." I promise you I was sober as the Judge I am four days a month, and no, the car was not moving. It all comes down to my having the physical grace of a hippo trying to pull off jazz hands in a minefield. I was wearing sandals, and caught my little baby toe on my left foot on the door frame on the way out.[5] Which ended up also being the way down. Like always, I was in a hurry, and didn't stop to assess the damage.

Until after I got home. At home, I took a step out of the car into my nice, level garage floor and it felt like I had stepped on live charcoal. I got inside and inspected my foot. It was nasty. Deformed, purplish-black, and looking more or less like it belonged in a leper colony, it was clearly damaged.

Still, I thought, it's a toe. What are they going to do? So I taped it up and went about my business.

More than a month later, it still hurt like the fire of a thousand suns if I stepped on it incorrectly. I mean, honestly, I have better things to do in my life than deal with a stupid little baby toe, so I kept popping Motrins

5. It is ALWAYS the left side as you will see later.

and taping it up and figuring it would eventually heal itself. Eventually the swelling went down enough for me to notice a little bump on the inside that felt like a bone poking in the wrong direction. That seemed terribly wrong, so I went to the podiatrist. He took an x-ray, and then announced that I had broken the little baby toe clean in half, and it was never going to get better so long as I kept walking on it without immobilizing it.

Enter the boot, the same boot[6] I wore when I last had metatarsalgia, because why not.

And it was on that boot that I strolled into Luke McFarland's grant-fueled writing class at Morgan County Middle School. I was actually invited as a sort of show and tell entity, the real-life version of what they had been learning about. Picture the shaky educational film narrator's voice saying, "Here is the elusive North American Drivel Writer, come out of her habitat to find a decent gas station in which to refill her coffee cup with writer fuel...see how her eyes dart independently from side to side as she..." and then the film breaks with that flip flip flip noise you can only hear in your head if you are over forty.

Anyway, because of the gas station coffee, I had to go to the little girls' room, and I asked one of the girls in the room where it was. She pointed next door. The school architect, from the firm of Goebbels & Goehring,[7] placed the girls' bathroom approximately 2¾ inches higher than the hallway, and tiled the elevated step with a special light deflecting tile that makes it impossible to see that it is a step. I lifted my foot in the traditional manner, intending to place it on solid ground in front of me and make my way in to the facilities.

---

6. Upon seeing my boot, my daughter put her hand on her hip and said, "Mom. That happened over a month ago. You are supposed to be taking care of me. How can you do that if you won't take care of yourself?" Sometimes she's wiser than she knows.

7. Or was it Torquemada & Sade? Or Howard, Fine, & Howard?

Instead of moving forward in the expected manner, the toe of my jackbooted foot caught on the lip of the step and I fell, face first, into the girls' bathroom of Morgan County Middle School, sliding forward about three feet before gliding to a stop like a curling stone, only without all those pesky aerodynamics and with fifty years' worth of accumulated ammonia and middle school girl shoe droppings instead of freshly swept ice in front of me.

I did my business, disinfected my entire body as best as I could in a bathroom with precious little soap and no paper towels, and went back into the classroom. I immediately told on myself which, I have to say, is an excellent ice breaker if you ever need to win the attention of a passel of 14 year olds. One sweet girl asked if I was hurt.[8] I said, "I think my knee is bleeding." I pulled up the leg of my pants and it wasn't so much bleeding as weeping, but the skin was definitely missing, probably ground into the fabric of my pants. Another girl got me a Band-Aid from the class collection. One boy, whose name is only a few letters shy of a celebrity crush I had when I was his age, thinking he was oh-so-funny said, "You're as agile as a cat with roller skates, aren't you?" Ha-ha, I thought. Mr. Cool Guy thinks he's so awesome. Well, guess what? I'm not the same girl I was when I was 14—I'm not afraid to own the awkward for a good laugh. "Rollerblades,"I said. "On a freshly oiled bowling lane. Being chased by a three-legged golden retriever."

Another boy, after offering me some of his Fuego Takis (which I refused) and part of his Reese's Pieces Peanut Butter Cup Super Candy (which I most whole-heartedly did NOT refuse) asked if I'd write about this incident and, when I said of course I would, he asked if I'd talk about him specifically. And so I am. Did. Am.[9]

I was there to talk about writing, and even though much of my time

8. The boys were just laughing. I don't blame them. It was funny.

9. If I were a real middle school writing teacher, I could tell you which one was correct.

was taken up with speaking of my adventures in clumsiness, I suppose I taught them all the best writing lesson I know: It's all material, even when, or maybe even especially when, your middle school nightmares come true.

This Is What I'm Asking For

I am under the (perhaps delusional) impression that my standards are fairly low. I don't think I ask for a whole lot. My rules in the house boil down to "Keep the dishes out of the sink," "If you're going to touch my stuff, put it back when you're done," and "Don't talk to me until I've had at least one and a half cups of coffee in the morning." My rules at work all boil down to "Do what you said you were going to do."

And yet, I am very often dissatisfied. It's gotten to the point where sometimes I am afraid to tell people what I want, because they can't disappoint me if I don't tell them. Which is the wrong way to look at the world, I know. I shouldn't let my fear of disappointment over-rule my ability to demand certain basic things. So, in an attempt to overcome that bit of psychosis, in the following pages I will try to make clear my expectations for people who interact with me. For the people who don't interact with me on a daily basis, I've tried to make my expectations entertaining and, possibly, just a little bit relatable. Here's hoping…

My Funeral

Right about the time I graduated from college, my friends started getting engaged. It got to the point where every week there was either an engagement, a shower, or a wedding. This was what my social life was: pretending to care when someone unwrapped a Mr. Coffee, elbowing other women wearing uncomfortable dresses out of the way for the bouquet, and secretly taking notes for my own celebration, which eventually occurred near the middle-end of this life stage.

This transitioned somewhat seamlessly into babyland. Someone is pregnant. Someone is having a baby shower. Someone has a newborn. Someone is having a first birthday party for someone who thinks you can eat cake by smearing it into your eyebrows.

For a while there was a lull. A few people got divorced. A few got married and remarried. Kids got Bar Mitzvah-ed. Some kids got married. Some people had grandchildren and had to decide if they were "grandma" "meemaw" "granny" "nanny" "nana" "gigi" "meemee" "nini" or any other made up combination of nonsense syllables that tries desperately to indicate grand-maternal pride while not sounding like a blue haired woman with a ratty shawl and an ear trumpet.

And then, right about the time I turned 40, it happened. A high school friend dropped dead. He wasn't sick that we knew of. He just, as they say, woke up dead one day. There was no car accident, no catastrophic illness he fought courageously—just the lightning strike of a heart attack and the rest of his life that would never be lived.

It threw me for a loop. I didn't know this guy well, but he was part of my childhood, and he wasn't older than me. He didn't have kids, which was a small blessing, but it made my own mortality come crashing down around me.

It's happened several times since. As a lawyer, I'm often one of the first people to know, because I have some practical knowledge about what to do when people die. But it doesn't make it any easier. I still get creepy Candy Crush requests from friends that have died, which is proof that you have very little control over who you send those things to. Funerals have become the new former-workplace reunions.

It's a kind of weird I still can't really wrap my head around. One day my friend is there, having lunch with me and making inappropriate jokes or talking about our kids, and the next day, she's not there, like some kind of irreversible magic trick. When I drive past their houses or workplaces, I find myself wanting to stop in and say hello, even though I probably wouldn't have when they were alive. Another weird thing about it is that, like I used to do with weddings, I find myself taking mental notes about what I do and don't want at my funeral.

So I'm putting this out there, here in this public forum, so there is no question. This is what I want (and don't want) at my funeral. And we all know by now that if you don't do what I asked you to do in the first place, bad things happen.

1. No one is allowed to talk for more than five minutes at a stretch. I don't want people's grief to be interfered with by hostile thoughts about when (or whether) someone will quit talking.
2. Extra bonus points for anyone who goes out of their way to tell a story about something we laughed about together.

3. Don't waste your money on enormous flower arrangements that will die in two days. There's enough death at a funeral without adding to it. If you feel the need to spend that kind of scratch, either send the flowers to a nursing home where someone alive can enjoy them, or donate the money to a cause that I'd approve of.
4. I'm all about music, but don't make everyone sit awkwardly while you pipe in what you think is my favorite song. I never know what I'm supposed to do during those musical interludes. I don't know what I'm supposed to look at or do with my hands. So I usually just look generally downwards and pick at my cuticles. I don't want anyone to have to feel awkward like that at my funeral.
5. Likewise, if there is a live singer, and they aren't capable of singing on pitch all the time every time, save it for amateur hour. This is MY funeral. There will be no shrill, sharp sopranos making my mourners' ears bleed.
6. No open casket. This is non-negotiable, and if you should happen to be there and see the coffin open, slam it shut for me. Remember the real me with bags under my eyes and my hair going in twenty directions, not some fake-waxy-faux-perfect version of me.
7. Don't feel bad if you find yourself laughing for one reason or another. I love gallows humor. My fondest wish is that something bizarre and AFV-worthy will happen at my funeral and people won't be able to quit laughing.
8. Make sure there is lots of food. Good food, too, not just a lame cheese-and-crackers tray and a half-flat bottle of Diet Coke.

That's a good, morbid start, no? I just hope someone can find this in

70 years or so when it is needed. Because for now, if laughter really is the best medicine, I'm going to live forever.

Bathroom Etiquette

As I sat down to do my business at work, I looked to the right out of habit and saw that there was a basic violation of bathroom etiquette: there were approximately one and a half squares of toilet paper clinging to a brown cardboard tube.

Something inside me snapped. This is a professional office. There are seven people who work here, with a combined total of thirty-five years of higher education between us. There is no excuse for this. I had visions of holding the offender's neck down with my foot as I scrubbed out his or her eyes with the toilet brush.

And as long as we're talking about the bathroom, someone needs to explain to me why there is EVER someone else's urine on the seat. If you sprinkle when you tinkle, please be neat and wipe the seat. You don't want to wipe it up because it's gross to touch pee? Well, guess what? It's TEN TIMES as gross when it isn't your own. My inappropriate vision on this one is with my hand on the back of the offender's neck, rubbing his or her nose in it like a disobedient puppy.

[Yes, his or her. We only have one-holers here in the office, and they are all first come first serve. Wanna make something of it, potty police?]

And more bathroom ranting: why should I EVER, in a public restroom, go in to a stall and see the fruits of someone else's labors. Flush. It. Down. If it won't flush, tell an employee. Yuck yuck and more yuck. (And pee-yew.)

I get that adulting is hard. Being responsible is a giant drag. I don't ever wanna. But I do. Because I live with other people and belong in a society which has to have rules. That whole golden rule thing? Do unto others, yadda yadda yadda? I take that kind of seriously.

As long as we're *still* talking about bathrooms, what is a grown up woman with a semi-respectable job supposed to say when she has to get up and go? That is, assuming something needs to be said. Having only recently come out of the life stage where there were small, impressionable children in my house and I had to watch my potty mouth (ha ha) I referred to it as "going potty." "Do you have to go potty?" "Go potty before we get in the car." "I have to go potty." I have so replaced whatever else I used to call it with the word "potty" that I can't make my mouth form any other words. My son, who is 14 as I write this, finds this unforgiveable. He chastises me for speaking to him like he's a toddler.

But what am I supposed to say? If I'm talking about myself, I can just be vague, like, "Excuse me for a moment." But how do I say to another mature human, "Do you need to go potty before we go?" And as I type that, I see the answer, plain and obvious. A mature human does not need to be asked. A mature human can suffer the uncomfortable consequences if he or she does not go potty before we go and can wait until we get there.

Of course, a mature human would neither pee on the seat nor use the last useable bits of toilet paper. Apparently there are not too many mature humans in my immediate orbit.

Sigh. What do I know? I just work here.

Introverts: Taking Over the World One Keystroke at a Time

I'm fairly certain that if you left me alone long enough I could take over the world.

Maybe that's why no one ever leaves me alone. They fear the conquering of a superior force.

Seriously, though, when I am left alone, I am a powerhouse. I can accomplish any task. If you leave me alone long enough, something is going to get cleaned, something is going to get baked, and a to-do list will be at least three-quarters scratched off.

Alas, the number of times in any given week I am left alone for more than ten minutes at a stretch wouldn't require you to use any toes to count. Probably not even your left hand or any fingers with rings on them.And for reasons I've never completely understood, when I am in the presence of others I simply can't get it done at the same rate.

There's a theory in particle physics which I only vaguely understand that says that the very act of observing something affects the outcome. I think that's my problem. When I'm being observed, the outcome is different.

I think this a problem for introverts everywhere. For us, other humans are like energy rods, sucking the energy in the room into their own orbits, to be used for their own purposes. Completely messing up the scientific metaphor here (bite me, literalists, even though I am one, usually) it is only when we are alone that our weak magnetic pull can draw the energy into ourselves enough for us to become productive.

This is why, conversationally, our wit sparkles when composed at a keyboard. We think of clever things to say, prepare beautiful turns of phrase, and make witty retorts and intelligent counterarguments. We can do this because we are the only real, live people in the room. Virtual people don't suck our functional brain energy away from us in the way that real people do. In person, we will think of the clever line about ten minutes too late when the timing is off. In front of a keyboard, I can dash off a Facebook response almost before the original 'speaker' has finished typing what they had to say in the first place.

People sometimes confuse our silence in crowds with shyness. And maybe some of us are shy, but not all of us. I'm not shy at all. I will talk to anyone about anything so long as I get the sense that the thing I'm talking about is remotely interesting to the person who is forced to listen to me. I don't mind talking in front of large audiences. If I know what I'm talking about, I'm not scared of saying it in any forum. To sum up, I can talk to one person, or I can talk to a thousand people. It's the in between that throws me off.

I can never quite get the rhythm of group conversations. I'm not sure if this is because of my innate lack of social skills, or the fact that I was brought up in a loud, New York, Jewish family in which everyone talked at the same time for efficiency's sake. I'm aware that what I consider 'normal' most people consider interrupting, and so I try not to. Instead, I turn over what I want to say in my head while the other person is talking until I have it just right and…by then someone else has jumped in the conversation and it has moved on and what I want to say isn't relevant any more.

Well, it's a good thing I have writing to save me, and a good thing

I'm at a stage in my life where I can call myself a writer without feeling like too much of a fake. Writing gives me my voice.

Now, please leave me alone for a moment. I have some writing to do. When I'm finished, then I will take over the world.

Ode to the Public Library

Every two weeks-ish I go to the public library to renew what I haven't finished, return stuff, and pick out more stuff. It's a place I pretty much take for granted. Every once in a while, though, the beauty of the place just knocks me over.

I don't mean the actual place. The building itself, named for the grandmother of a friend of mine who donated the land, is a kind of non-descript white concrete building of the type only built by governmental authorities. If it didn't have a sign in front saying it was a public library, you would still assume it was a public library because there is nothing else a building that looks like that could be.

But anyway, the boringness of the building's architecture aside, the inside is absolutely amazing. There is a whole bank of computers in there, at which—FOR FREE—you can write your Great American Novel, search for a job, apply for colleges, or do research for your homework. And the books? Unless you're like me and bring them back late all the time, with nothing more than proof of your address and a promise to return them they let you just take them for a couple of weeks. And then a couple of weeks more. And then a couple of weeks more after that. And if you're late, like I am embarrassingly often? I have to give them a quarter per book per day. A QUARTER! You can't even get gum for a quarter anymore, unless you are willing to settle for that rock-hard tooth-breaker stuff you find in questionable gumball machines.

There's free story time for kids. There's a chess club. There's the daily paper, local and semi-local and not local at all. Magazines. DVDs. Large print books, and books you need extra strong reading glasses to read. It is one of the few things that government consistently does right. It is a great equalizer. It gives anyone who wants it free access to useful resources.

The public library I usually go to is pretty user friendly. I don't actually have to go in there to renew my books. I can call or do it online. But I always go anyway. One reason is because I have this stupid, irrational dislike of the telephone. I also forgot my password for the website and have no idea which of my twenty emails I used to sign up. But the real reason is because nothing gives me more pleasure than walking amongst stacks of books.

Really, it's foolish for me to check out books from the library. The stack of books in my three to-be-read piles (I have to have three because my ceilings are only so high) contain so many volumes that if I did nothing but read between now and my ninety-fifth birthday I might maybe get to half of them. But I can't help it.

First I check the new releases, fiction and non-fiction. Then I wander through the stacks, checking out biography, humor, and fiction with more care than the other sections. I wait for a volume to call to me. Sometimes nothing does, and then I'm free to work on my stack. (An aside: I'm pretty sure those books next to my bed reproduce at a rabbit-rate when I leave them alone. There is NO WAY I've had time to buy that many.) But sometimes I hear it, that faint, desperate, "reeeeeeeead meeeeeeeeee" and I am powerless to resist.

So I check out my new book friend when it asks me to. And feel pressured to read it quickly because I have to return it on time so it can call to someone else who is as psychotic as me.

And if I don't, I pay a quarter.

That, my friends, is a bargain.

The Queen's English

I have a semi-well-deserved reputation amongst my friends as being a high-ranking official in the local branch of the grammar police. It is true that I have very strong opinions about the Oxford comma. It is also true that a misplaced apostrophe will actually peel the enamel off of my teeth. I worry over obscure and hair-splitting things like whether or not to say "the myriad ways things are done" or "there are a myriad of ways in which things can be done."[10] I'm enough of a fan of the Queen's English that I even prefer the superfluous "u's" that British people tend to use - like in flavour, harbour, and honour, though I draw an imaginary and irrational line at "colour."

One would think, especially because I just began this sentence with the word "one" instead of the more colloquial "you," that I would then be a purist when it comes to vocabulary. This is not true. At all.

If you have read more than, say, three of my blogs, you will know that I make up words with reckless abandon. This is largely because I am lazy,

---

10. Feel free to shoot me an email at lori@loriduffwrites to discuss your opinions on this matter. Don't be afraid to feel embarrassingly passionate about your opinion. I'm with you. Really, I am. But only if you insist on using the word 'of.' The dictionary disagrees with me—it says that 'myriad' can be a noun or an adjective. But it irritates the tar out of me when 'myriad' is used as an adjective. I can't justify this. But why must we always justify our feelings? Isn't it enough that our feelings are sincerely held?

but also precise at the same time. I know there is a very specific word out there that means exactly what I am trying to say, but I don't know what it is. A word that 'almost' means what I am trying to say will not cut it. I could pore through dictionaries or thesauruses (thesauri?) to find out the correct word, or I could just make one up.

Like, for example, the word "sploop." This is a measurement. And also a verb. It is the amount of semi-solid stuff (like maybe cookie dough or whipped cream) that comes splooping off the spoon when you give it a hard shake. You know exactly what I'm talking about, right? And if I hadn't explained it, but had just used the sentence, "I put a piece of pie on the tray, and ladled out a sploop of ice cream to go on top," you wouldn't question the meaning either. (Now that I've written all of that, I suppose that "dollop" is a better—and real-er—word that says the same thing. But honestly, isn't "sploop" funnier? And doesn't it capture the falling motion and the sound effect better than "dollop" does?

I also make up numbers and expletives. You might not know exactly how many zeros are in a squizillion, but you know it is unfathomably large. Likewise, if I am putting together a piece of Ikea furniture, and can't get the flippinflappin snÖrg marked "A" to fit into the kienwåčl marked "B" properly, you'll know I'm not paying it a complement.

Often, Yiddish will serve me when English does not. And, here in the deep south, with the exception of just a few of us, I may as well have just made up what is a real word. I use "schmatta" a lot. "Schmatta" literally translates into something like "rag" but it is used to mean a shapeless and/or poor quality garment. "Are you going to wear that schmatta?" Why, yes. Yes I am. It is warm and comfortable and I don't care what I look like.

This is all in contrast to my day job, in which I get to use words that are in fact real, but not recognized by Microsoft Word which, I think, has a setting for all manner of languages, but not "Legalese." Words like "hereinafter" and "wheretofore" and "whenceforth" get that red squiggly line underneath them. I feel like a high school English teacher is carving bloody rivulets into my writing. But I'm RIGHT! Doesn't that count for anything? And, as long as we're on the topic, Bill Gates, or whichever of his flunkies is in charge of such things, "therefor" is a completely different word than "therefore" and you need to quit it with the autocorrect.

The other day at work, I had to type the perfectly legitimate legalese word "usufruct" over and over.[11] I may use that next time I need to have a made up dirty word. It sounds seedy.

I'm completely fine with words like "gonna" and "ain't" and "aiight" because, while not exactly the Queen's English, they set a tone and a mood that "going to," "are not," and "all right" do not.

It's all about communication. If you know what I'm talking about, and there is no room for misunderstanding we're all good, made up words or no. That's why I insist on the Oxford comma. If I said, "This blog is written in honor of my English teachers, JK Rowling and Maya Angelou," you might think that JK Rowling and Maya Angelou were my English teachers. If I put a comma after "Rowling," you will know that I'm talking about my English[12] teachers AND JK and Maya.

So, say what you want to say. Just be clear about it. And, for the love of all that is good and holy, do not use an apostrophe for a plural.

---

11. A 'usufruct', in case you cared, is a kind of life estate in property—you get to use it while you are alive, but after you die, or after a precipitating act designated in the usufruct, you have to pass it on to the—I swear this is the proper term—'naked owner' intact. It's hardly ever used, and then only in Louisiana.

12. Yes, I am talking about my English teachers, not my "language arts" teachers. Don't get me started, especially if you refer to yourself as a "media specialist" instead of a "librarian."

Drag Queens, Candy Crush, and Mental Sorbet

When I get home from work I am tired. Between the drama that is work, and the drama that is headline news, and the drama that is mothering two young teenagers and a retired husband, the last thing my brain can handle is anything of substance.

I like mind candy. Escapist fiction. Stupid comedies on television. A little mental sorbet, if you will.

My tastes vary, and are usually a few years behind the times. I find shows years after everyone else did. Recently, I watched a random season of *RuPaul's Drag Race*. For those of you even more clueless than I am, RuPaul, drag queen extraordinaire, hosts a reality show which pits aspiring drag queens against each other in different competitions. At the end of the show, the bottom two performers must "Lip Sync for their Lives" to see who will be eliminated. It is high camp. I love it.

It makes for fun, stupid conversations with my family. For example, what would your drag name be? After some thought and discussion, I finally landed on Acid Reflexxx. (I ultimately rejected "Strep Throat," which was in the running for a while.) I shall use lots of acid green, sparkly eyeshadow. Another close personal friend, who shall remain nameless, decided upon "Patricia Vagenstein," which makes me giggle every time I think of it.

What's your drag name?

Really, these Queens are rather talented. They are designers and seamstresses and dancers and choreographers and models and makeup artists.

What I like best about them is their attitudes. No doubt they get a world of hurt from family members and their communities and the world at large. People aren't always very nice to other people who aren't mainstream. Boys in lipstick don't always—or ever?—have an easy time in high school. But they get out there, and they strut it like they mean it and, well, good for them.

What I like about the judging is that it isn't really a beauty pageant, though it might look like one at first glance. Attitude matters more than cheekbones. "Chunky yet funky" Latrice Royale (my personal favorite) is just as beautiful as thin and glamorous (and disturbingly Cher-like) Chad Michaels. You are rated on your creativity, your confidence, and your ability to walk wearing five-inch stilettos and a three-foot hairdo. Not your genetics. Not your willingness to starve yourself. It's what you do with what you have, not what you have that matters.

Which is a fabulous attitude, is it not? Everything I needed to know I learned from drag queens. Don't worry about whether or not your butt looks big in that dress. That's not the right question. The question is: can you rock it? Can your attitude demand that people admire your curves?

Of course, I don't always have access to drag queens, and sometimes I don't even have the emotional energy to get invested in an episode of reality television. There are times when their relentless energy exhausts me simply by looking at it. Comes the end of the day (defined on some bad days as 3:00 p.m.) and I can be completely brain dead. There has been enough input and the overworked filing clerks in my skull need some time to sort out the information gathered in the day and put it into some sensible order.

Enter another form of mind candy. I fought Candy Crush for a while because I know that it is an A-Number-One time waster. There is nothing of much value to it. It doesn't solve any problems, or accomplish anything useful. At best, it's a test of your spatial reasoning, but that's quite a stretch, and not the kind of stretch that produces lovely salt water taffy. But here's what it does: it is a useful meditative tool for those of us who are incapable of sitting perfectly still with only our thoughts to entertain us. It gives my fingers and my eyes something to do, while not requiring much of my brain so it can go to its metaphorical room and shut the door and think about what it has done that day.

It also gives teeny-tiny rewards. I may not have accomplished anything else today, but by gosh and by golly I got past that monstrous level 679 or whatever it was. Plus? That guy who says, "Delicious" in that low, sexy voice? (You know, the dude who was probably paid a hundred bucks about ten years ago for five minutes of voiceover work to record "Delicious" "Sweet" "Tasty" and "Sugar Crush" but whose voice I would recognize on the street more quickly than I would recognize my own mother's?) I live for that guy's praise. When that guy tells me what I did was "Divine?" Well, at least I know someone appreciates what I've done today.

I also like collecting Bears in "AlphaBear" and building castles and cathedrals in "Triple Town." And adding my squares up to 2048 in the game creatively named "2048." I like "Words with Friends," but, honestly, it's too much thinking for most days.

All of which is insane. I don't have time for this. At any given moment, there are six or seven things I need to do for my kids before the next school day, four hundred zillion undone projects on my desk at work, articles to write, toilets to scrub, dishes to do, bills to pay, and the other myriad of responsible things responsible grownups are supposed to do.

Nearly every moment I spend not doing those things I spend listening to the mosquito-pitched disapproving voice in my head. (Why wasn't there a 'guilt' character in "Inside Out"? I'm guessing because Riley wasn't Jewish like me or Catholic like my husband.) This voice is a nasty bully, the kind I'd make my children stay away from. "Lazy. Lazy lazy lazy," she says. "Get off your fat butt and do what needs to be done." She doesn't let me rest, that Guilt-witch. It's better I listen to Mr. Toffee, or whatever the deep-voiced Candy Crush guy is named. He's nicer to me than I am to me.

So. To sum up. I'm not lazy, no matter what the voice in my head says, and although my butt may have a little more padding than is optimal, my failure to raise it out of a chair from time to time means only that I am getting the rest that I need. Real candy has a purpose: it is a little bit of pleasure with no value other than that it is pleasurable. There is nothing wrong with pleasure for its own sake. It doesn't mean that you don't eat broccoli and choke down kale, too, it just means that now and again, eating a Snickers bar isn't going to kill you and might actually cheer you up. You eat candy as a treat—mind candy is exactly the same. As long as it doesn't replace essential nutrients, who cares?

This is true. You can take it to the bank, or my name isn't Acid Reflexxx.

The Ice Cream Man

At first I didn't notice it. There are so many background bells and whistles these days that it kind of blended in. But it was persistent. I thought it might be someone's ring tone. The sound was travelling—getting louder as it approached. Then it dawned on me. A fake calliope version of Turkey in the Straw? It was an ice cream truck.

My office is in the back of an office condominium complex. There are fourteen or so brick buildings housing lawyers, insurance agents, accountants, doctors, dentists, and the like. Real grown up businesses that do boring, somewhat unpleasant, but definitely necessary things.

And there was an ice cream truck. Driving through our parking lot.

I shot up out of my chair. I yelled, "There's an ice cream truck!"

Diane popped out of her office. "Really?"

"Yes," I said, and pointed out the window at the white van driving slowly.

"Little Lady!" Diane shouted, and we hurried to get the young daughter of a colleague who was here after summer camp. "I-c-e-c-r-e-a-m?" I said quickly to her mother, so in case it wasn't okay there wouldn't be a tantrum. "Ice cream?" said the overly-precocious little girl. Mom sighed in resignation.

Diane ran outside to make sure that the truck would wait for us. I grabbed up Little Lady and ran as fast as I could in two inch heels.

Turned out the running was pointless. There was a line of professional people wearing professional clothes lining up to get their Rocket Pops. The ice cream truck wasn't leaving our parking lot any time soon. One man, wearing pressed pants, wing-tipped shoes, a white dress shirt, a tie, and a lanyard with an ID card around his neck, jumped up and down, making fun of all of us and himself at once. "The ice cream truck is here! The ice cream truck is here!"

I laughed.

I got a Strawberry Shortcake. Little Lady got an ice cream sandwich. Little Lady's Mom got a Neopolitan ice cream sandwich. Diane got nothing because, well, she's Diane, but we love her anyway.

Little Lady's grin was huge. My grin was huge. We were all immensely happy. It was about seven thousand million degrees outside. The ice cream cooled us down and tasted wonderful.

I handed the ice cream man a twenty. He was a tattooed millennial with one inch gauges in his ear. Little Lady was eating her ice cream beside me making happy noises of the kind that you can only make when you are six years old without getting sideways glancing or someone, referencing *When Harry Met Sally*, wants to have what you're having.

For a brief, fleeting moment I looked at this guy, wearing his "I Put Ketchup on my Ketchup" t-shirt and thought how much I hated gauges and how they looked trashy and wondered what his Mom thought. *At least he has a job*, I thought.

Then I realized this guy had figured out something huge that I hadn't. And he'd figured it out at a young age. All my degrees and fancy clothes, and very few people like to see me coming. On the other hand, people jump up and down and literally run across parking lots making fools of themselves to get to him. He's got a job making people happy. And he can wear comfortable clothes while he does it.

To heck with the law degree and uncomfortable clothes. I want to be an ice cream man.

When Mommy Gets Sick

The heat finally broke here in Georgia, meaning it isn't 80 degrees out before sunrise, and also meaning that I get my annual season-changing illness. I get sick every October, this one being no exception. I went home from work early on Friday and, more or less, have been in bed ever since.

This is a large statement, whether you realize it or not, on the intensity of how lousy I feel. Mommy doesn't have time to get sick. I power through most things. But I couldn't power through this one. Friday afternoon I fell asleep, face down on the bed, wearing a full face of make-up and a lawyer-appropriate dress. When my daughter got home from school, she dropped her normal hard crunchy exterior in favor of her soft, chocolatey middle and took care of me. My bones were chilled. She brought the electric blanket I bought her for Hanukkah over to me, draped it across me, and plugged it in. She made me a mug of tea. Then, with my permission, she left to watch her brother's marching band dress rehearsal.

I woke up long enough on Friday to drink a glass of water and eat some Trader Joe's Chocolate Cat Cookies, the only things in my pantry that didn't make me bring up bile just by looking at them.

Saturday morning I managed to get up around 9:00 a.m., feeling more or less refreshed after that much sleep. Not healthy, but much much better. I went to QT to get coffee and supplies, dropped Jacob off at the high school for his marching band competition, and then went to the car wash Marin's Girl Scout troop was doing to raise money for the special needs cheerleading program at the school. (They didn't wash my car so much as smear the dirt around and get it wet, but, well, it was for a good cause, and so I thanked them profusely for doing such a great job and gave them twenty bucks.)

As a purebred Jewish mother, I know that nothing knocks out an illness like chicken soup, so after my car was smeared I headed to the grocery store to get ingredients. I also got some orange juice and fresh fruit, including some amazing looking giant honeycrisp apples. Honeycrisp apples, when fresh, are so good they are probably the variety of apple that was growing in the Garden of Eden. I could see giving in to that kind of temptation, even with a no-no warning from God. They are also stupidly expensive. I bought six of them. They were $15.00. The chicken for the soup—an entire animal, plucked and processed and gutted—was only $9.00.

By the time I got home, I realized that I wasn't quite as healed as I thought I was, and the thought of doing what I needed to do before I could get to bed was overwhelming. But I am nothing if not a fighter, so I pushed myself to put away the groceries and make the soup. As I lifted the bag of apples to put them away, in my bacteria-laden fog I lifted it upside down, and the apples went tumbling out. Into the dishwasher, which was open because it was clean and drying out. Four of the six apples impaled themselves on forks. I wish I had the presence of mind to take a picture—I could not possibly repeat this. The other two bounced off the edge of the dishwasher and rolled all the way across the nastiness that is the kitchen floor. All the apples had holes or cuts in them. $15.00 worth of apples, ruined.

I knew what had to be done. I didn't want to do it. But I washed the apples and cut them up. I got out the crockpot, found sugar and cinnamon and ginger and butter and made stewed apples. When life hands you ruined overpriced apples, make a dessert.

Come to think of it, make a dessert anyway. Dessert is the best.

As is chicken soup. If you want my recipe, you can have it—it's in my last book, "You Know I Love You Because You're Still Alive." (See what I did there? #ShamelessSelfPromotion) I made the soup, leaving the mess on the counter to deal with At A Later Date, and crashed again on my bed for six hours.

And when I woke up, I had soup. And stewed apples. I drank two bowls of soup. I don't know if it was the hot soup, but the fever come back, or a hot flash. I started sweating so much it was dripping off my elbows and soaking my shirt. So I took a cold shower.

And now I'm exhausted again with all the effort of eating and sweating and showering. But my tummy is happy, and I have hope for the future. Chicken soup will do that for you.

Maybe next time, someone will make it for me.

White Hat Hacker

I have a website. I'm proud of it. You can find it at www.loriduffwrites.com. I paid someone to set it up initially, but ever since the very beginning I have changed it and added to it often. It's one of my children, really, lovingly created out of materials I had on hand. It is very meaningful to me.

To me, anyway.

I get that it is not likely to be meaningful to any other human being on the planet. As things go relatively in the world, it isn't very important. You can't purchase the necessities of life on my website, or get information with which to do your homework or write your dissertation, you can't edit photos or meet new friends. (Unless, of course, you take one of my classes, or get into a very interesting conversation in the comment section below, all of which I urge you to do.) The world turns, people are born, they marry, and they die, all without interference or help from my website. It's not even as important as mosquitos, since it isn't on anyone's food chain. The world is not better or worse because it exists. The world is, more or less, indifferent.

Which is why it surprised me so much that I got hacked.

I checked in on my website, much like you might check on an infant to see if it is breathing, for regular feeding and maintenance, and I found this:

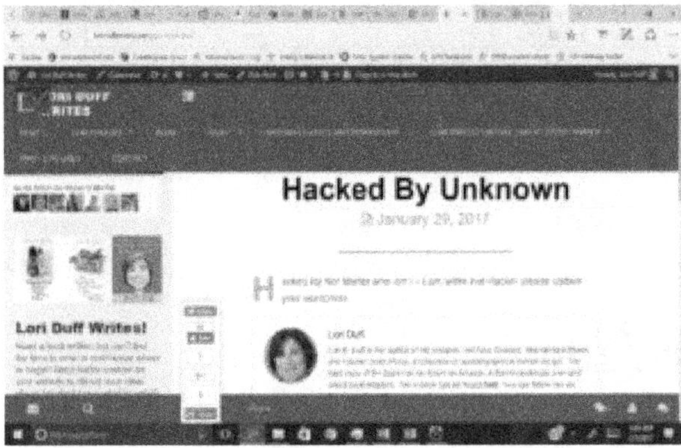

That particular page should have looked like this:

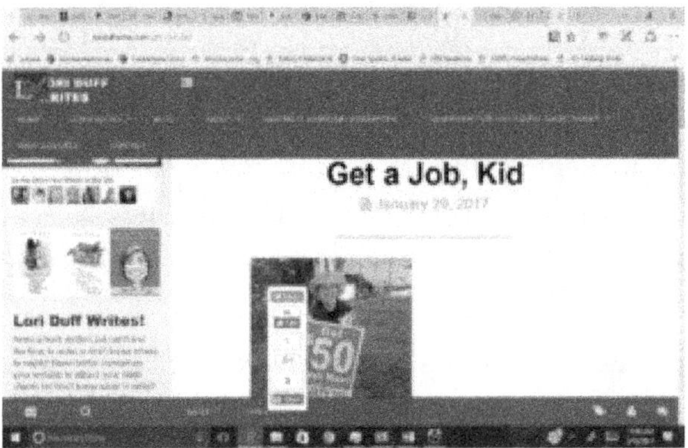

I was NOT a big fan of the switch, largely because I had not done it, and no one else has the password to do it. The text I DID NOT WRITE, unlike the million other words on the website, told me that the evildoer was someone or something called "white hat hacker." This sounded like a Batman villain to me, one who shopped for cigarette holders with the Penguin.

I Googled "white hat hacker" to see who else was the victim, and learned that "white hat hacker" is a category, not a particular person. A white hat hacker is a hacker (in my head I go with a stereotyped slightly overweight, pasty-faced, acne-ridden white male aged 17-23 whose only romantic relationships and actual friendships have been with virtual people, and who desperately needs a haircut) who hacks into websites for allegedly benevolent reasons. They hack in and make themselves known in order to alert people to security problems.

I *think* that's all my hacker was doing. It was an easy fix, all I had to do was click "restore previous version" and confirm that I did, in fact, want to restore the previous version of the page. I updated my WordPress, like the hacker suggested, and I have not noticed any other problems.

It was annoying. And scary.

And, in an odd way, extremely flattering. I know I'm not anything more than dust in the wind. My life and my brain droppings are important to me. I have trouble believing that there is anyone else in the multiverse who would give any more than a two second "awww" if my website ceased to exist. It would take a very long time before most people—including my family—even noticed.

But a white hat hacker noticed my existence, and for the moment I will take him at his word that he only means to help. I'd like to return the favor. Mr. White Hat Hacker, if you're out there somewhere, let me know who you are and I'll help you with your grammar.

Where are the Sponges?

A few times in my lawyering career, I've had medical malpractice cases in which careless doctors accidentally left things in people's bodies after cutting them open. Wires, superfluous body parts, and the ever-popular surgical sponges, to name a few. I get that carelessness happens. I've been known to be careless from time to time. I have a giant wad of keys, the likes of which would impress any elementary school janitor. I only actually use two of the keys and one of the key tags, but I've learned that if I have a giant wad of keys I tend to know where its big, jangling self is at any given moment. If I just have a couple of keys, they get lost. I lose things all the time. I've left credit cards at restaurants, I leave my carefully packed lunch sitting on the kitchen counter, and I've left socks and toothbrushes in hotel rooms.

So I get it. It's easy to lose things. I just think, if you've got a human being flayed open in front of you, that a quick inventory of the things you put in there would help you keep track of the things you took out. If I leave my phone sitting on the bathroom counter at the gym and never see it again, I just go to Verizon and get another one. It's semi-annoying and may cost me a few bucks, but it isn't really a life changing thing. Having a pair of clamps floating around my abdomen might make a bit of a bigger difference in the long run.

I recently went to the hospital to visit a friend who had just had a baby. (Cute baby, by the way. Tiny little thing. Smells like milk and poop.) Being a lawyer, and therefore being hyper-aware of liability issues, and being a nerd who actually reads fine print, and being a humor writer who lives for finding odd things in unexpected places, I looked around the hospital room while it was someone else's turn to hold the baby. There were two posters on the wall, warning posters, which caught my eye.

The first was a brightly colored poster titled "Where are the Sponges?" Apparently, it is easy as 1, 2, 3 to find out where the sponges are. One should inspect the sponges before they get put into someone's body, they should be counted, and when you're done, there should be the same number of sponges as sponge holders. Well, that's great, I thought. And really freaking obvious. But what good is this poster in an obscure corner of a mother and baby room? Shouldn't it be sterilized and hung somewhere in the operating room? The couch it hung next to was designed for visitors like me, people most unlikely to leave sponges inside of their friends.

But that's not all. Someone somewhere decided that telling someone with seven years of post-secondary education how to count in 3 easy steps was not sufficiently complicated. Another, bright yellow poster was hung next to the first one. It had several different checklists for different people—surgeons and nurses, and gets more technical about x-rays and additional help—but really comes down to the same basic advice: count. What goes in, must come out. One should, as the poster advises, "Pause for the Gauze."

Again—great advice! But how many surgeons are standing in a back corner of the mother-and-baby rooms to get surgical advice? And how many surgeons have you met that would think for ten seconds that a poster could teach them anything? I've never even met a surgeon who thought another *surgeon* could teach him anything.

Mainly, I'm concerned that this is a big enough problem that it deserves cutesy posters placed all over the universe like so many handwashing signs. I saw more don't-leave-sponges-in-people's-bodies posters in the hospital than I've seen anti-bullying or drunk driving posters in my son's high school.

I'm not sure what my point is, other than I found the placement and existence of these posters entertaining in my weird, twisted little way. But, you know what they say: A Poster A Day Keeps the Lawyers Away. And no one likes to see lawyers coming.[13]

13. Except, of course, everyone on the planet who has had a worse-than-average day. Make all the lawyer jokes you want, but seriously—who is the first person you call when the poop hits the spinning fan blades? You don't have to like us, but you do need us.

First World Problems

So, I get it. I have a comfortable income, an intact marriage, two healthy children, and two living parents. I don't live in a war zone and no one in my family is in jail. When I wonder where my next meal is coming from, the question comes out more like, "Do we want to order food from the Chinese place or the Italian one?"

My problems, or at least the ones I'm willing to share in public, are the epitome of First World Problems. The word 'problem' is a huge exaggeration. Still. We've all had pebbles in our shoes and noticed that those teeny-tiny little rocks can really affect the trajectory of our days. My point, in writing about these pebbles, is not to insist that they are boulders, but rather to share the universal experience of pebbles, hopefully in a way that makes you giggle. Laughing, I've found, not only dislodges the pebbles from your shoes but wears down boulders if you laugh hard and long enough.

Here's to the magic powers of erosion.

Uphill in the Snow. Both Ways.

I'm not sure when exactly I got old enough to begin every third sentence with "when I was a kid," but seriously, folks, when I was a kid, things were different. I could go on and on about technology, and how I had to type out my college papers on a typewriter and then retype them after edits were made, but I won't. I won't talk about busy signals on phones or even the concept of an expensive 'long distance call.' I won't mention the three television channels, and the rabbit ear antennas with the foil balls on the top of them, or the weird yoga poses you had to maintain in order to get a consistent signal.

Nope, I'm talking about the ability to put one foot in front of the other and travel more than 50 feet without whining.

My children won't walk anywhere. Granted, the place where we live is not an especially walker-friendly place. There isn't much of anywhere to walk, and there aren't many sidewalks. Still, the skill is the same as the one that takes them from their bedrooms, where they watch hours of Netflix, to the sofa in the living room, where they also watch hours of Netflix.

We went to Chicago back in October for my cousin's wedding. I was excited to take the Dufflets to a big city, and to show them what sort of freedom they would have if they could just walk a few blocks to an overpriced coffee shop instead of having to beg for a ride there. They liked that part. But when I suggested (and insisted upon and actually executed) a mile and a half walk to our destination upon sidewalks designated for that purpose and with lots to see and do (and eat) along the way, there were more tears than on the actual Trail of Tears. Okay, maybe not literally, but there was more whining.

I have to say that this whining is kind of state sanctioned. Over a decade ago, when I had to commute into Decatur every morning, I often got stuck behind a particular school bus which stopped three times in about 100 yards. You could see the first bus stop from the third bus stop. The kids looked to be high school aged to me—they weren't five year olds. I thought that was the beginning of the end of society as I knew it, and I might have been right. It was explained to me that since the road was a big one (it was) and since there were side streets that had to be crossed, for liability purposes they had to make the three stops. I did not mention (okay maybe I did) that perhaps when I was in fifth grade I had to cross a six lane divided highway without adult supervision in order to get to school because my house was within the mile and a half limit where the bus wouldn't get you. But still, this is the age of lawyers, liability law suits, and no personal responsibility whatsoever, so, as the kids say, whatevs.

This year, however, I regularly get stuck behind a bus that is even worse. This is a middle school bus, which means that the youngest person on it is about 11. The first time I got trapped by the incessant stopping I almost stroked out. It stopped at a driveway. Kids got off. Then it stopped at the next driveway, which was not twenty feet away from the first. More kids got off. Then it stopped at a third driveway, another thirty feet down the road. It skipped a driveway, then stopped at a fourth. I sat behind the bus, (im)patiently waiting, lawfully obeying the stop sign arms, sucking in diesel exhaust fumes for probably ten minutes. If my blood pressure could have been harnessed, I could have powered a small city for an afternoon.

I mean, SERIOUSLY. These were not baby children. I will grant you there were no sidewalks, but the only lawn that needed to be crossed was their own. There were no streets to be crossed. The road itself was small, and barely wide enough for two lanes of traffic. This is INSANE. I mean, completely, absolutely, and without reservation INSANE. Back in my day (insert shaking fist and clicking dentures here) my high school bus had ONE BUS STOP. We all crossed streets, walked, trudged through snow and sub-freezing temperatures (in the dark) in the winter, to all congregate in one place so the bus only had to stop once.

Conventional wisdom is that millennials are the entitled generation, spoiled rotten and expecting the world to make things easy for them. Well, why wouldn't they think that? Haven't we taught them the truth of that assumption? Everything is instant and on demand, and they don't even have to walk next door to get to the bus.

When I was a kid? We would have insisted on walking up hill. Both ways. In the snow. Just for the sport of it.

Men, Women, and the Functionality of Pockets

There will never be true equality between men and women until women have functional pockets in their clothing.

Hear me out.

I recently had the tremendous pleasure of meeting Dr. Gina Barreca at the Erma Bombeck Writer's Workshop in beautiful, sunny Dayton, Ohio, where apparently it can snow sideways in April. Dr. Barreca is the author of "If You Lean In, Will Men Just Look Down Your Blouse?" In this book, Gina (I can say "Gina" instead of "Dr. Barreca" because once you've worn a Mardi Gras mask and cussed in front of someone, all formalities go out the window) says, among other tidbits of wisdom: "Not only do women hold up half the sky; we do it while holding a 500-pound purse."

Gina says it is because we are caretakers, and if you ask us for a Band-Aid, we will ask you if you want a big or little one, latex or fabric, etc. Whereas if you ask a man for so much as an aspirin, he will wonder why you are asking him.

But *why* is this? Is this because of some innate need we have to take care of everyone around us and make sure that they have everything that might be required in any eventuality? Maybe. I'm not a sociologist, and I haven't actually studied this phenomenon, but that doesn't stop me from having opinions and drawing conclusions and telling you what they are.

I think it is because of pockets.

We don't have useful pockets.

All you really need when you go anywhere is your cell phone, your driver's license, a credit card that isn't maxed out, and a twenty dollar bill. If you don't live in a place with public transportation, you need a place to put your car key. There are few situations that these items won't cover. All of these things fit neatly into the back pocket of your garden variety pair of jeans or khakis, or even men's dress pants.

But not the pockets in women's clothing. These things, when they even exist, are shallow and useless[14]. You might could fit a breath mint in some of them. I'm told this is because of a woman's curves: because our bodies tend to be rounded, putting things in pockets would make for weird lumps and shapes in our clothing when we want them to lie flat.

I've got news for you, honey: ain't nothing you're putting in or on this body gonna lie flat, whether or not there's a credit card inside it. There's not a flat plane to be found. And besides, we all expect to see a rectangular lump on the butt cheek of a man where his wallet regularly lives. No one judges the quality of his posterior based upon that, not that we should be looking, anyway. Can't we have the same expectations for women?

So when you have a bag that you're toting around, it's easy to just throw one more thing in, just in case. Once you've filled your pockets, you've filled your pockets. You can always get a bigger purse.

So back to the conference. I wanted to travel lean. There was no reason to drag my 500-pound purse (which, when you are a Mom and your

---

14. When I first typed this sentence, I thought of a thousand conclusions to it: shallow and useless…much like the Kardashians. Much like most politicians. You get the drill. But I try to be nice and make fun of only me in my writing. I try. There is no benefit in hurting the feelings of a real human being for nothing but a cheap laugh. But oh the temptation…

kids still live at home, is 750-pounds) around to seminars. But I had no pockets. I couldn't find a good solution to where to put my money, my credit card, and my driver's license. I transferred it back and forth between the ID badge holder, the conference tote where I kept my materials, the few outfits I had with functional pockets, and stuck between the pages of whatever book I was toting around like a fan girl trying to get the author to sign. (Yes, my luggage was 74% books I wanted to get signed by various faculty members, 17% hair product and makeup, and only 9% clothes—with no pockets. Wanna make something of it?)

I'm generally a systematic person. I like for things to have their place, because then I don't have to look for them because there is only one place they will be. With no system, I don't know reliably where anything is. And I lose things.

So I lost things. Like my driver's license. And I had to fly back home in a post-9/11 world.

When I got to the Dayton International Airport to fly home and went to pull my driver's license out of my jeans pocket, I couldn't find it. I looked in the front pocket of my travel backpack, which is where I usually put all my purse-related items when I don't have a purse or a functional pocket. It wasn't there. I looked everywhere I could think of, and I couldn't find it.

This is a real problem when you want to get on an airplane.

I dug through my wallet to see what was in there. I found my ID from the City of Loganville, where, believe it or not, they let me be the Municipal Court Judge. It had my picture on it, so I stepped forward to the front of the line and hoped for the best.

I spoke quickly, and all in one uninterrupted word."IDon'tHave-MyDriver'sLicenseIDon'tKnowWhereItIsAndIDidn'tRealizeItWas-MissingUntilTwoMinutesAgoIDoHaveThisAndItIsGovernmentIs-sueDoesItCount?" I tried to look as pitiable as a person can without holding an actual sad puppy.

Thankfully, I got the laugh I was going for, and the woman behind the counter said, "It should be okay, if you have something else with your name on it. Where's your boarding pass?" I pulled out of my wallet three different credit cards, my library card, and my health insurance card. Then I looked in my left hand where my boarding passes, newly printed out from the electronic kiosk, should be. They weren't there.

"I don't know where my boarding pass is," I said, trying hard to look like a person who could possibly hold the title of responsibility on the ID I was trying to pass off as mine. (It was mine. I am normally responsible. I promise!) I looked around at all the flat surfaces surrounding the place where I had my initial moment of driver's license induced panic. Seriously. How far could this thing have gotten in the twenty feet I'd walked and three minutes since I printed it out?

"Do you need assistance to the gate?" Asked the woman behind the counter. She winked in an understanding, we've-all-had-these-days kind of way.

Eventually my boarding pass was located on a counter I swear I hadn't stood at, the TSA/Homeland Security equivalent of "TOTAL LOSER" was written on it with a Sharpie, and I was pointed towards security. I was warned that I'd probably have to have "additional screening" but beyond that it should be okay.

When I got to the front of the line, there was a chain of people who yelled "Alternate ID" like a fire brigade, and I was eventually passed to a very professional female security guard who unpacked my laptops from my backpack, and fed everything through the x-ray machine for me. Clearly someone who couldn't find her driver's license on the day she had to fly was not capable of such complex tasks as putting a backpack on a conveyor belt.

I was brought over to a rubber mat and told, essentially, that I was about to lose my virginity in public, and if I wanted to, I could go in a private room. I said no, because I'm frankly a little bit afraid of private rooms operated by the federal government, and because I really really just wanted to get a bagel and coffee on the other side of the security gates in as little time as possible. I said, "You can do whatever you want. I'm just excited you're going to let me on an airplane."

After we rounded third base, my new suitor wiped a little pad thingie all over her rubber gloves (always use protection) and stuck it in a machine. The machine told her that I was not, in fact, coated in explosives. Then she rubbed a little pad thingie all over my cell phone and my laptop and stuck it in the machine. The machine told her that they were coated in explosives.

Excuse me? I don't even use expletives in my writing, much less explosives on my laptop.

A supervisor was called over, and my cell phone and laptop were taken away to who knows where to be further screened. I tried to look baffled (which was easy) and casual (which was not.) What is the etiquette when one is suspected of bringing an explosive laptop on an airplane? I believe I used my talents as a wordsmith and said, "Seriously?"

Whatever it was, the second screening said that I was safe, and I was sent on my way without so much as a fake phone number and a promise to call real soon.

I'd never been so relieved to have the privilege of spending $6.00 on a stale bagel in my life.

P.S. I later found my driver's license stuck in the pages of the program booklet for the conference. Which WOULD NOT HAVE HAPPENED had all my clothing had functional pockets.

Dress Code Blues

Once upon a time, I gave birth two and a half weeks early to a little six and a half pound peanut whose legs were so scrawny that even preemie diapers wouldn't give him a snug fit around the thighs. Through a careful diet of fruits, vegetables, lean proteins, and Cheetos, over the years that boy has grown to nearly six feet tall with size 12 feet. Last night, I took that boy to his freshman orientation at high school.

"You're old," he said. "You have a kid in high school."

Well, maybe that's true. I didn't have a kid when I was in high school or even in my 20s—I was in my 30s when he was born, so I am definitely older than the average mother in our community. They handed us a booklet when we walked in. They herded us into the gym and then proceeded to read the booklet to us, with special emphasis on the parts that said, "if you screw up in 9th grade, you're going to be sorry in 12th when you still have to make up for it."

A lot was said about the dress code. I don't envy the good folks who have to come up with a dress code that is reasonable and promotes modesty without being sexist or overly puritan. Especially when they have to compete with the buyers at major retailers who (apparently) refuse to sell shorts for girls with an inseam longer than three quarters of an inch.

I admit to being a little bored, and I admit to running out of lives on Candy Crush fairly early on in the evening, so my mind wandered a little and I got to thinking about the dress code. I had come to the orientation from work and was still wearing my work clothes. That day I wore a dress made of a bias cut knit chock full of spandex because I am a curvy girl. Tailored fabrics without give don't work for me. The dress went down to my knees and up to about three inches below my neck. It was not form fitting in any way. I thought it was rather conservative.

According to the letter of the dress code, however, it wouldn't have passed muster. "No spandex skirts" said the dress code. Oops. "No visible cleavage." Double oops. Not that I was hanging out or anything, but as a well-endowed woman, unless I'm wearing a turtle neck, the very top of the girls can be seen.

And so, because I am me, because my job has ensured that I know everyone in charge of things, and because there is nothing more entertaining to me than humiliating my son in public places, I marched up to the School Resource Officer. "Does what I'm wearing violate the school dress code?"

"I…uh…uh…in what way?" He said.

(Right about this time, my son melted into the crowd, disappearing from sight.) "The spandex skirt." I pulled on my skirt. "The one inch of cleavage." I pointed at my cleavage. This made him uncomfortable and he looked away.

"I…uh…uh…Hey look!" He said. "Dr. Nobles!" He called over the assistant principal who was in charge of such things.

I repeated my question. "Does what I'm wearing violate the school dress code?" She, too, asked in what way, and I repeated my demonstration.

"No, no," she said with a face like I was talking crazy talk. "We're talking about those short little tight skirts. And v-necks where you're spilling out."

"That's more like it," I said, relieved that lawyers hadn't gotten involved with nit-picking the precise language of the dress code in the way that we would the Official Code of Georgia.

"Be careful what you say," said the Resource Officer, "Or you'll end up in one of her books."

"I'd be honored!" Said Dr. Nobles. "You can quote me."

And so I did. And I didn't get suspended or anything, despite my spandex skirt and cleavage.

As a self-employed person, I get to set my own dress code, which is codified thusly: "Whatever I think is appropriate and has no visible stains or odors." And, although as a blanket rule that works for me and my co-workers, I admit to following nonsensical societal rules about dress codes.

I am writing this on September 22, 2016 which is, so the calendar says, the first day of fall. It is approximately ninety-jillion degrees outside and, to be honest, inside my office, since my law partner thinks anything below 80 on the thermostat means we are trying to freeze him out. If you spend too much time in his office, you start smelling bacon when your salty-from-schvitzing skin starts to cook.

But outside, it is still summer, regardless of what air conditioning could do for us if we let it and regardless of how the Earth tilts on its axis relative to its position around the sun.

If the leaves are changing to brown, it is because they are dying in the heat.

All of which is a long and winding lead up to this: why can't I wear white pants? Why can't I wear linen? Because some unnamable person, probably a society person who belonged to some kind of members-only club that wouldn't let me in, both because I'm a woman and a Jew, decided that once Labor Day hit, white pants were a sin on par with adultery and taking a penny without ever leaving a penny in the little cup by the cash register.

I actually looked it up to see if there was some reason, and even the people with an actual budget for such esoteric, useless research like staff reporters for *Time Magazine* couldn't find a consistent explanation amongst fashion historians. And as long as we are talking about actual budgets, who pays fashion historians to be fashion historians? That doesn't seem like the kind of career goal that would allow you to pay both rent and groceries. Although now that I think of it, given the waif-like size of your average fashionista, maybe groceries aren't so much a priority.

But me? I eat groceries, lots of them, and I have a few natural layers of insulation that make warm temperatures a little bit trying. Plus, I'm a sweater. I don't glisten or shine or perspire. I sweat buckets of rank, briny fluid that drip with audible plops and stain my clothing and make people do that flared nostril, pinched mouth thing they do when they are pretending like they don't smell an inhuman stink coming from someone who otherwise looks like a professional grownup.

Not that white pants are the answer to my troubles. But they HELP. Light is no more than visible energy. White reflects light and the heat associated with vibrating energetic molecules away from me. Darker colors collect it, turning my pants into Thermoses, keeping the hot things hot. Plus, I like my white pants. They look good with patterned shirts. They happen to fit me well. And I can usually go three quarters of the day before dropping some colored stain-inducing food on them.

The bigger question, the meta-question, if you will, is why I care. I am 46 years old, and I'm pretty confident that the color of my pants isn't going to determine whether or not my life is ultimately a good one. I guess it is because I am a rule-follower. I like rules. As someone who often feels socially awkward, when I know what the rules are I will follow them no-matter-what because that's one less reason for someone to exclude me from the cool kids table in the lunchroom. (We never get over the fears we had when we were 13, do we?)

As problems go, it's not a big one. No one is dying or crying, only whining. There is no great injustice anywhere: there isn't and shouldn't be any #WhitePantsMatter movement.

But really. Whoever it is that says that you can't wear tails on your suit coat before 6:00 p.m., or velvet after Valentine's Day, or socks with sandals (okay, maybe that last one does make some sense) can you PLEASE reverse course and change the rule to allow me to wear white pants so long as the temperature is hot enough to boil the water in the bottle I left in my car?

Please? Pretty please? For me?

Been There, Done That, Got the T-Shirt

Generally speaking, I'm not a big fan of stuff. Stuff is just clutter. I want to get rid of stuff. I'm not particularly sentimental, although I do have trouble getting rid of stuff with faces. Photographs, stuffed animals, even Happy Meal Toys. Their little eyes just look up at me from the trash can and my heart breaks.

Back when I used to have time to sit still and watch television, I would make little crocheted stuffed animals for friends when they had babies. I thought they were cute, even if no one else did. Part of the creation process involves scissors and stabbing the half-made critter with needles. Which was fine—it was just yarn and fluff. Except that once I sewed on a face I felt like I had to be nicer to it.

Back to the point, I don't really collect things. I should say, I don't really collect things that aren't useful. I have ended up with a whole lot of coffee mugs, which appear more regularly than I can break them, which is sadly often. I use these coffee mugs to drink the magic bean potion that gives me life every morning.

I also realized recently that I collect t-shirts. I have what seems to me like upwards of seventy million t-shirts. I have so many that I have to keep some in the hamper at all times because I don't have enough room to put them all away. Everywhere I go, everything I do, there seems to be a t-shirt to mark the occasion. Most of them have dates on them and a description of the event. Some are cuter than others, but they all trigger memories.

Some of them are really old. Like high school old, keeping in mind that Ronald Reagan was president in my high school years. This means, quite literally, that some of the t-shirts I actually wear (even if it is just to bed) are older than my kids' teachers. It used to irritate me when people who were older than me said things like, "I have socks older than you." But the truth is that I do have some vintage '80s slouch socks that are, in fact, older than you. Well, maybe not *you,* but *you* over *there*.

A good number are from college, most of them marking things my sorority did, like rush and our annual Twister tournament on the quad. Every time I put one on I think of my sisters, and maybe how we argued over the design of the shirt. I have one from rush from 1990 (which I know because it says 1990) which makes me think of Gerry Rogers every time because she drew the giraffe on the front.

Lots of my t-shirts are new, or new-ish. The latest addition to my collection is from the Loganville Police Department's "Donut Dash[15]," a 5k race, the proceeds of which go to support the Special Olympics, an inarguably fabulous cause. I didn't run, or even try to mosey the 5k, mainly because it started at 7:00 a.m. and I'm just not getting up early on a Saturday. But I did donate enough money to the cause to get my name on the back of the t-shirt, which is how I earned one. The one before that was an Emory Alumni shirt, given to me when I was in the Emory Alumni tent at the Decatur Book Festival.

You could probably take all those shirts and line them all up (assuming you had enough football fields in which to do so because seriously,

---

15. Is that not the most fabulous name a police department could ever have for an event? The logo is a donut with legs and a police hat. Love people with a sense of humor.

we are talking about a LOT of shirts) and get a pretty accurate picture of who I am. You'd know where I was and when. You'd know what causes I support. You'd know what size I was at any given moment. (Answer: XL, except for a brief period in the mid-90s when I was a medium.) You'd know I've been there, I've done that, and I got the t-shirt. I've thought about doing one of those quilts, but I don't know how I'd narrow my choices to 16 t-shirts.

Every once in a while they wear out, and that's sad. They get so holey they are useless for anything but a dusting rag. Right before that point is when they are at their peak—soft and worn, there is nothing better to sleep in. But I guess t-shirts have to wear out, or there wouldn't be room for new t-shirts.

Not that there's much room now. I've got a lot of memories.

No Fair! Or, More Whining about Inequality Between the Sexes

"No Fair!!" (stamps feet like a toddler)

Anyone who tells you life is fair is trying to sell you something. This is not news to me, or anyone else who has spent more than, say, four years on planet Earth. But still, it's a human need to fight injustice wherever we see it. We may not be able to balance the scales, but by God we can do our best to quit from tipping them over.

I'll be the 4,261,366th person on the internet today that will say that one of the greatest causes of cries of "no fair" is gender. Boys earn a dollar for every 75 cents a girl earns. Studies show that boys get more attention in school. Boys can become professional athletes, or even get jobs commenting on other boys who are professional athletes. Girls? Occasionally. Not so much. I mean, go ahead, name a rich, professional female athlete that ISN'T Venus or Serena Williams. I dare you.

It costs more to dry clean a woman's shirt. Shampoo in a pink bottle is more expensive.

Men can unzip and relieve themselves more or less anywhere in a matter of seconds. Women have to wait on line in order to lock themselves in a tiny, unsanitary room and then undress themselves by undoing complicated undergarments and then packing it all back together.

I could go on. And others have.

But seriously? The whole of life's unfairness came crashing down on me this morning when I took my son to the dermatologist to get Accutane. Accutane is a drug that you take for about six months, and once you take it, you never have acne again. They don't dispense it like Pez in middle school cafeterias because it really is a dangerous drug. It can wreak havoc on your liver, so you have to get your liver enzymes tested monthly. It can cause mental health issues. And it can cause birth defects like nobody's business.

But it only messes with the reproductive systems of girls. It is the kind of medication that comes with a book—not a booklet—and a million paragraphs you have to initial that basically say that if even if you aren't a girl and you are on Accutane and you get within 100 yards of a woman who might become pregnant sometime within the next five years, that woman will birth a swamp creature.

There's a flowchart in the book. One side is for girls who might get pregnant one day. The other side is for boys and girls who can't get pregnant because those boys and girls might one day ride in a car with a girl. The boys' side says to get your meds every thirty days and don't donate blood. The girls side has four times the words, and may as well just say, "Abandon Hope All Ye Who Take This Medication."

Seriously. Look at this:

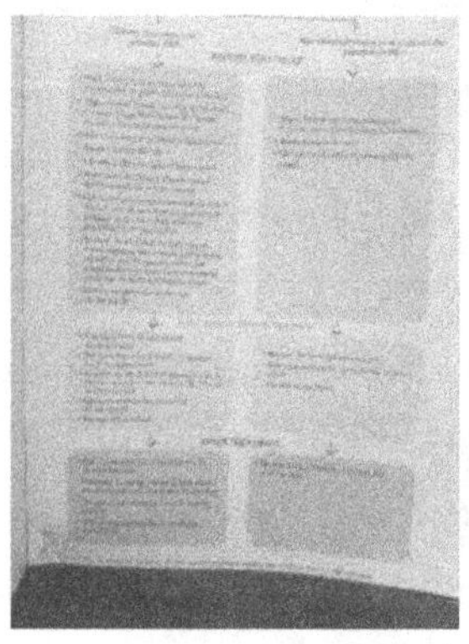

It's okay if you can't read all the words. The point is not the words themselves, but the number of words. Life is simpler on the boys' side.

If this isn't an analogy for everything that is wrong with the structure of the universe, I don't know what is. Because it isn't sexist. Boys and girls simply have different parts that play different roles in the reproductive system. There is nothing any shift in attitude or change in legislation can do to make there be an equal number of words in each column. This is biology, baby. It's science. It's true whether or not you believe in it.

And believe me. It is NOT FAIR.

The Joy of Accidental Discovery

I took my children to the public library not too long ago. I am lucky that both of my children like to read, although my daughter is generally pickier than my son about what she will read. Neither of them particularly like library books, because, so they say, they are convinced that everyone who has borrowed the book before them has coughed and sneezed and dripped their lunches into the pages and, well, yuck. Easy for them to say, since they don't have to pay for much, and they know I am a sucker for buying books. I feel like denying my children something good to read is as close to child abuse as denying them green vegetables. Personally, as I've already mentioned, I like the library. I like wandering the stacks, waiting for the joy of accidental discovery on the spines.

I like checking out new treasures at the library, particularly the books on tape, which are not books on tape, they are on CDs or are MP3s, but I am old and I can't change the phrase in my head to "audiobooks." I have made amazing finds there just wandering the shelves. So I took my children there one day, because they were in the car, and they had no choice.

My daughter remembered something she wanted to read, and stood helplessly in the middle of the stacks. "How do I find what I'm looking for?" she asked.

This made me very sad, and I admit that the ancient, creaky phrase "card catalogue" slipped through my lips before I dragged her over to the computer to show her how to search for the book. She found it, went to the shelf where it was supposed to be, and that was that.

It got me to thinking about search engines, and how much easier it is to find what you are looking for on the computer than it was to walk your fingers through yellowed cards, soft with age and everyone else's fingerprints.

But it also got me to thinking how you only find what you are looking for.

I mean, I do like the dictionary on my Kindle. I like being able to point to a word I don't know and get the definition right away, so I can read on and move on. But I also like getting out the giant unabridged dictionary I keep on a shelf in the living room. It makes my children roll their eyes when I say "let's see" when they ask me what something means. I thwomp the book on the dining room table and leaf through the pages to find what we are looking for. They can NOT understand why I don't just tell them, or why I don't Google the answer or ask Alexa. I think they are kind of surprised that I didn't just check with Google to find out what their names were when they were born.

The answer is always there in the book. So many other things are there, too. If you look up the precise definition of "contumacy[16]" (to pick a random word that happens to be on a piece of paper near me as I type) you will also find "contumely" and maybe "consummation" or "consommé" along your way there.

Back in the day, when the word "google" was always paired up with "eyed," and you wanted to look something up, you went to the encyclopedia. And more often than not you'd spend a million years looking for it, because some picture of a really gross looking fish would catch your eye, then maybe you'd look at the dinosaurs, then maybe you'd get around

16. Merriam-Webster says contumacy means, "stubborn resistance to authority." Which, since I'm talking about my kids, is a perfect word to use.

to looking up whatever it was you went to look up. Granted, I was a nerd-child (who has grown into an unrepentant nerd-adult), but I remember spending many hours just thumbing through the encyclopedia finding random things.

Same with card catalogues in the library. You'd pull out the long drawer, looking for something to help you with your social studies project, flip-flip-flipping the cards, and along the way you'd find a card for a book that seemed even more interesting.

The only way my kids will accidentally discover anything interesting is if they misspell whatever it is they are looking for and the misspelling happens to be something else. Everything else is algorithm-ed directly to their demographics, browsing history, and blood type, for all I know. These kids don't even see ads that aren't related to something they have already looked at or spoken about when Siri was listening.

So, they'll find what they want. They'll find it quickly and efficiently, and then they'll move on to the next task.

How they'll ever feel the joy of accidental discovery, I'll never know.

My Love Affair with Piles of Books

None of us know exactly how we are going to die, but if I had to take a guess now it would be that I'll get crushed to death under a pile of unread books.

I have piles of unread books everywhere, though I promise you they are organized in my fashion. The books I've read and want to keep are on bookshelves, classified by genre, then author, then publication date. I can find any book I've read in an instant if no one has moved it which, in my house, is like a 50/50 proposition, because there is something about a part of the house looking neat and organized than makes the household gods crazy and compel someone to touch it and destroy it. The ones I don't want to keep are either given away or traded in at the used bookstore.

I have a real compulsion about buying books. I find them everywhere. I've found great books in the dollar store, at yard sales, at Goodwill, at library sales, and, of course, on the internet. I love discovering authors no one has heard of before, which is easy to do if you troll the indie books Facebook pages like I do in the hopes that while I'm stalking someone else they will also find me. If I find an author I love, I will instantly buy all their books, even if I know it will be years before I read them all because I really don't like reading the same author's books in a row for fear that it becomes too much of a good thing.

Overstuffed bookshelves, to me, are the pinnacle of the decorative arts. My dream house might or might not have a home theater in it, but it definitely has a two-story open-ceilinged library with exposed beams and one of those ladders on wheels. There are enormous overstuffed leather chairs to curl up in under a soft blanket when I read. There's dust in the beams of sunlight, but there's always going to be dust with that much paper in the room.

If I go to your house, and you have a bookshelf on display, I have to look at it. I mean, I have to, in the way that I have to breathe and beat my heart. I will make assumptions about who you are based on the books on your bookshelf. For that matter, if there are no books visible in your house, I will make assumptions about that, too.

Honestly, I think I've shed more tears over fictional characters than I have over the real people in my life in the past ten years. That probably doesn't say anything good about me, but facts are facts.

I'm usually in the middle of several books at a time. I listen to audiobooks in my car, and I count that as reading. I have at least two on my bedside table, one serious and one light, depending upon my mood. There is usually one in the living room next to the La-Z-Boy for the five minutes a week in which my living room is quiet enough for me to get my read on. And then there's my Kindle, which usually has at least two books open at a time, one of which has been for the past few years and will be for the next few years, a book in the *Outlander* series, which, considering they are like 1000 or more pages each and I don't often read my Kindle, may never ever be finished. Which is okay, since I'm kinda in love with Jamie Fraser and don't want to say goodbye to him. (The other one at the moment, in case you were wondering, is the *Kura* by Mary Patterson Thornburg, another of those indie authors I was talking about above, one that no one knows about but should.)

I always read the book before I see the movie, which means I am rarely going to like the movie, because the characters always look wrong. Two notable exceptions: *Harry Potter* and *The Fault in Our Stars*. Even though Isaac was way wrong in *The Fault in Our Stars*, Hazel and Gus were dead on, so it was okay.

I try to keep up with what my kids are reading, which is nearly impossible now that my son has figured out how to keep a book on his lap during math class and he reads approximately seventy zillion words a minute. (I'd get mad at him for reading during class, but the kid has straight A's, so…) That's just as well, because I find that Young Adult literature is often more imaginative and interesting than the blah blah blah same old same old fill in the blanks and change the names tripe written for real grownups.

Truthfully, I can't understand how anyone gets to sleep without reading a few pages of a book first.

I'd go on, but I can't. I finished two books yesterday, and there are about six in the pile next to my bed competing for who gets to be next. I need to go mediate the situation before War and Peace breaks out.

Metatarsalgia and Me

If I don't die as a result of being crushed under a big pile of unread books, another likely fatal event is my refusal to go to the doctor because I think the doctor might think I'm just a whiner baby. Honestly, I don't know why I care so much. I'm sure no one at the doctor's office does. They get paid either way, and if there's nothing wrong with me, they don't have to do much.

Of course, because of this stupid policy of mine I don't tend to go to the doctor until things are really, really bad, and so I have never gone once when they said there was nothing wrong with me.

Two days ago, my left foot (I told you these things always happen to my left side—my left wrist broke, my left foot had a bunion, my left eye had a cataract) started swelling like I was nine months pregnant. Some might argue that my belly did the same, but that was a long time coming, and was traceable to several years' worth of desk jobs, meals-on-the-go, and Dairy Queen Dilly Bars. The foot was sudden. The feeling was somewhat familiar. I remember my tootsies being so swollen while pregnant with my daughter that the only shoes I could fit on my fat little feet belonged to my husband. When I walked, the liquid in them sloshed, and you could see waves of fluid crashing over the top. It was gross and uncomfortable, but worth it when you see how smart and kind and funny and beautiful my daughter is.

This, however, was not the result of a pregnancy, and was sudden onset and very uncomfortable. The skin felt stretched and sore. The next day, every time I took a step it felt like someone was digging their elbow into the top of my foot. I imagined the worst—foot cancer, blood clots, flesh eating virus eating me from the inside out—but knew it was probably nothing.

So I checked with my primary source of medical pooh-poohery, my friend Diane, who is most famous for telling her son to suck it up and wrap his broken hand in an Ace bandage before finally relenting and taking him to the doctor five days later. I figured if Diane thought I should go to the doctor, it was probably sound advice.

Dr. Diane diagnosed me with a hairline fracture and said I should go to the Orthopedic Urgent Care clinic and get a boot to walk around in for a few weeks.

With her hard-to-get blessing, I went to the clinic. They took me in to x-ray my foot, and I felt the need to justify my being there. I blathered on to the x-ray technician. "It's just weird, it doesn't hurt that badly, just in a way I've never hurt before, so I thought I'd get it checked out, it's probably nothing, but look, it is swollen, it looks weird and gross, see? My other foot doesn't look like that." I looked down, and worried that maybe my other foot did look like that. I don't have pretty feet. I have large slabs of meatloaf with little stubby piggy toes.

The technician kindly humored me, and took pictures from all angles, then shuffled me into a room to await the verdict. I sat there with my foot not hurting at all because I was sitting still, feeling like a fool for being there.

Finally, the P.A. came in and told me that the x-rays looked fine, but they could see the swelling on the x-rays. (Yes! Justified!) She said I probably had something called "metatarsalgia" which is a word that trips so poorly off the tongue that I have to say it with a space between all the syllables. It means that the heads of the bones in the front of my foot, just before my toes, are inflamed, probably for no reason at all, although it could be from a whole lot of running, which I assure you in my personal case it could not be. Although it is probably overkill, the best way to get rid of it is to walk around in a boot for a couple few weeks and rest it as much as possible.

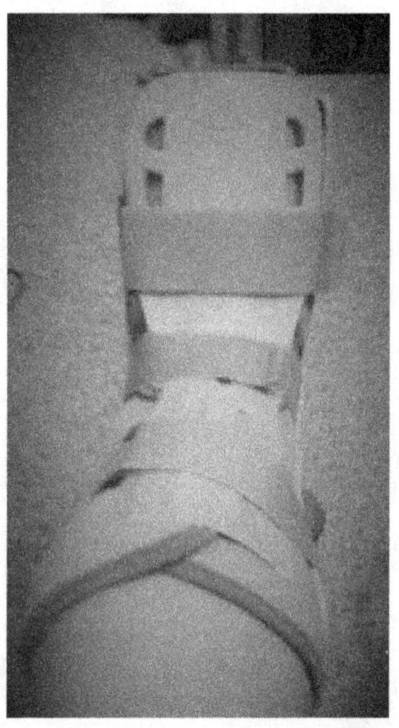

Sometimes I think these things are God's way of telling me to slow down.

I'm not that thrilled with the comfort of the boot, nor with the boot as a fashion statement. It is approximately 763 degrees in the shade here in Georgia in June, and there is some serious rankness that goes along with wearing a padded boot and a long sock in this kind of weather.

Still, the boot is a great big physical manifestation of the fact that there is indeed something (physically) wrong with me, and I'm not just a whiner baby. About this, anyway.

Hello, Alexa!

Why did I buy Alexa? Well, holiday gift giving in my house is always tough. There are the teenagers who are guaranteed not to like whatever 'thing' I buy them: simply because I chose it, it has to be uncool. Gift cards are workable, but not much fun to open. As for my darling husband, he has at least six of everything he could ever want.

There's plenty of stuff in my house. Too much stuff in my house. We need to get rid of stuff, not add to the mix. Which is tough to square with wanting to be generous and whatnot.

So I was excited when I discovered the Amazon Dot. For only $40.00, I could get a device which, if it worked, would kind of be like Siri for my house. None of us are techies. Few of us can operate anything more complicated than a doorbell with any kind of fluency. But it was worth a shot, and I couldn't think of anything else to get my husband.

Turns out, this thing is AMAZING and so easy to use even a Duff can set it up. And no, I am not being paid to say this, though if the good folks at Amazon wanted to reward me for this by promoting my books, I would totally let them.

We're still figuring out what it can do. It links to an app on my phone, which I have learned the hard way to check with some regularity. Right after we got it, my daughter said, "Alexa," (the Echo Dot goes by Alexa, and you have to say her name to get her attention) "Buy me a TV." Alexa told her what the most popular TV bought on Amazon was and then asked if she wanted it. My daughter said, "Yes." Alexa said, "Okay." And we all had a good laugh. A few minutes later, my son cautiously said, "Alexa, cancel my previous order." And we forgot about it.

Until I got a notice a few days later that they were sorry the TV was going to be at my house after they promised it, but I should expect it on my doorstep tomorrow.

Oops. I should have known that Amazon is not huge on confirmation steps—I accidentally published my first book as an e-book, chock full of typos, because I expected there to be more "Are you really sure? Click yes? No seriously, are you sure?" screens.

But I'll forgive Alexa that, since it was user error, and she did helpfully allow me to buy more Polaroid film without me having to write it on a to-do list or boot up my computer. I didn't even have to quit doing the dishes.

Alexa plays whatever music we want her to play. She tells us the weather. She tells us horrible jokes that make us laugh stupidly. ("What kind of movies does the printer like?" "Paper view!") She plays *Jeopardy!* with us, and pretends to be the Sorting Hat from *Harry Potter*. She wins about half the time when we play *20 Questions*. She can predict the weather with as much accuracy as anyone else[17]. She wishes us a good night and a good morning. If you buy the right appliances she will turn them on and off. The other night I said, "Alexa, play music that doesn't stink." And she said, "Here's a mix of songs I think you will like." And I actually liked them! I asked her to do the laundry and, while she refused, she offered to buy me laundry detergent.

No thanks. I'm still paying for that TV. Plus, due to the kind of buy-one-get-one free type sales at Publix that gets my husband into raptures, I think we have 75 bottles of detergent in the basement.

---

17. Including a Magic 8-Ball—I know meteorology is supposed to be a science, but I swear the plate in my wrist is a more accurate predictor of rain than our local weatherdude.

I would think Amazon should give these devices away for free, since it makes Amazon Prime a must and shopping is dangerously easy. I'm sure it does a thousand things we haven't figured out yet. My daughter worries that perhaps Alexa is more interesting and personable than she is.

I guess in some ways I should consider it creepy. My husband doesn't like to say certain things in front of her for fear someone is listening. My personal opinion is that anything said in my house is so boring and unimportant that if there really is someone on the other end listening, having to listen to all that nonsense is probably punishment enough. I'm actually okay with sharing certain information so they can tailor what they try to sell me to my personal tastes. It saves me from uninteresting ads.

Besides. Alexa is a kind and benevolent overlord, who only has my best interests at heart. At least, that's all I'm willing to say out loud inside my house.

Pollen Season

I have a superpower. I can take take in nutrients via ordinary grocery items, like lettuce and milk and Little Debbie Snack Cakes, and turn them into pounds and pounds of pollen-induced mucus. I can do this without, apparently, expending a single calorie. It is the one thing at which my body is remarkably efficient. I do this at such a rapid rate that I can go through an entire box of tissues in a day. If it were somehow a cash crop, I would be a millionaire.

The constant sniffling makes everyone ask if I'm crying. Which I sort of am—there is extra fluid in my eyes in my body's attempt to wash the invaders free.

Few things are as physically beautiful as spring in the deep south. Loud pinks and purples, buttery yellows, whites that catch the sunset, and firey reds decorate azalea bushes, dogwoods, cherry trees, redbuds, wisteria, and honeysuckle. There are flowers everywhere. The air smells like a subtle dessert. It smells like sneezing. Yup, it's pollen season.

I made a decision years ago that the only color car I would buy was a yellowish gold. Pollen colored. Otherwise, it would be a sickly green color in the spring like everyone else's.

People think us southerners are exaggerating when we complain about the pollen. And maybe we do, a little, but the truth is that there is so much pollen it gathers in drifts like snow. You can scrape it off your windshield in handfuls. You can try to use your windshield wiper fluid, but probably you'll just end up making an opaque paste and smearing it across your field of vision.

Seriously: this is a picture I took outside my office:

Back when I wore contact lenses, I couldn't wear them in the spring. I may as well have just stuck Velcro in my eye for all the comfort I felt. My eyeballs felt like a hoard of miniature porcupines had taken up residency and were scratching out a place for themselves. Now that I've had eyeball surgery and can see unassisted, my eyes are merely red. No matter what, it looks like I've had a hard night of drinking behind me. When it is really bad, my lower lids look swollen and bruised, as if I'd been on the losing end of a bar fight.

We can't eradicate pollen, and we don't want to. Unlike mosquitoes, pollen has an actual valid purpose. Pollen is, I know, the way flowers and fruits grow. Without it, there'd be no roses and no tomatoes. Love is, quite literally, in the air during pollen season.

But really. Can't love get a room?

Eyeball Surgery Redux

If you've read my books (and I'll pause here while you go order them off of Amazon or the online retailer of your choice if you haven't) you'll know that I have a pretty lengthy history with eyeball surgery. As a person too blind for Lasik, I got implanted contact lenses which involved slicing open my eyeball and shoving a permanent contact lens in there. Then I got a cataract in my left eye and had to have the permanent contact lens removed, along with the lens I was born with, and replaced with a lens that looks more or less like a hat a member of the band Devo would wear while whipping things, whipping them good. This resulted in eyeball stitches placed oh so delicately two days before I coughed my head off from pneumonia. But really, read my books for the whole story(ies.) I'll wait[18].

The cataract lens worked for a few years, but then I started getting bleary. From the inside, it looked like a movie camera trained on a 1940's starlet, smeared with Vaseline for romantic effect. So, back to the eye doctor I went.

I was told that my situation was not uncommon. There is a membrane that lives behind where the cataract lens was placed and sometimes that membrane doesn't like the cataract lens, and you get depos-

18. Yes, I am aware that this is nothing short of shameless self-promotion. But seriously? I don't see you shamelessly promoting my books for me, so someone's got to.

its; or, as my grandmother would say, because many times Yiddish says things better, "schmutz;" on the membrane, clouding one's vision.

No biggie, I was told. We just zap them with a laser.

No biggie to YOU, I thought. See, having my eyeballs zapped with a laser is something I've had done before. Back before I had my implanted contact lenses put in, I have to have holes zapped in my irises to avoid the buildup of pressure. The answer to the question you haven't even formulated in your brain yet is: yes, that is approximately twice as uncomfortable as it sounds. Maybe three times. Maybe seven.

But I survived it, and I'd survive this. This one was easier, I was told. I didn't even need someone to drive me. Mmmmmmmhmmmmmm.

At the appointed time, I went to the surgical center where the laser was located, and got only one eye dilated as big as a dinner plate[19]. My pupil was so large, I was afraid to look down lest my brain slip out of the opening.

Eventually I got called back, and I sat in a chair opposite the kind of head and chin strap contraption that only eye doctors, Nazi scientists, and dominatrixes[20] would ask you to put your head in. The doctor sat on the other side in what looked like one of those pre-virtual reality video game consoles where the chair swings along with your fake laser gun when you move. Only this wasn't a fake laser gun. And he was aiming it at my poor eyeball.

"Pew! Pew!" said the laser gun, as it zapped away the gunk from the back of my eye. I heard and felt a crackle with each shot, not exactly painful, just odd and unpleasant. "Pew! Pew! Pew!" said my eye doctor, clearly having too much fun. "Ah! That one almost got away! Pew! Pew!"

---

19. There's an 'effacted and dilated' childbirth joke in here somewhere, but I can't quite work it out.

20. Dominatrices? Dominatrii? Leather-clad scary ladies?

I began to hum the theme song to Super Mario Brothers, the only video game theme song I could conjure up under the circumstances[21].

And that was it. I was given a pat on the head and sent on my way. I prayed hard I wouldn't get pulled over, since it would be hard to explain my oddly uneven pupils without the assumption of methamphetamines or maybe some off brand LSD getting in the way.

But guess what? I can see now. Through both eyes. Thanks, doc, for beating the boss level monster with your special laser gun!

21. As I sit here now, unencumbered by terror, I can also conjure up the theme song from "Tetris" and the "Act One" and "Act Two" songs from Ms. PacMan.

Sleeping with a CPAP

Along with age comes wisdom. Also, extra body fat, wiry chin hairs, and an inability to distinguish one pop song from another. Me, I got an extra bonus—the ability to snore. I snore loudly and dramatically, so I'm told. My snoring is so intense that it actually affects the atmospheric pressure of the house, making the walls bow in and out like in a Tom & Jerry cartoon.

And so, after threats from my family that I would be forced to sleep outside with the coyotes, I went to the sleep doctor to see if there was something that could be done.

At first, I was given a sleep study machine to take home. It consisted of an elastic belt with sensors, a little clip for my finger to see if I was getting any oxygen from my struggles, and a cannula, which, for those of you who didn't learn that vocabulary word from reading *The Fault in Our Stars* by John Green, is a little plastic tube that has spikes that fit in your nostrils. Cannula are *usually* for shooting oxygen into your nose, but in this case they were there to measure what my honker was sucking in and shooting out all night.

Not the greatest way to sleep.

But, the results came in. Apparently, I stopped breathing about 35 times a minute, and my oxygen level got down to about 75%. I had moderate to severe sleep apnea.

No wonder I was tired all the time.

So I went in for a sleep study at the sleep clinic. I got there in the evening, and changed into my pajamas and brushed my teeth. A tech glued sensors all over my body and fit me with a mask before tucking me into a big, fancy hotel-style bed. I admit I felt a little awkward. The tech was a young guy, probably on the 'not quite' side of 30, friendly and chatty, and just good looking enough to be distracting. He was kind enough not to make fun of the fact that I brought my teddy bear for a familiar comfort. I felt like an old, lumpy fool in my flannel sleep pants and t-shirt dating back to the Clinton administration, smiling and nodding as he explained what he was doing.

I tried not to think about the fact that he was being paid to watch me sleep. I tried to remind myself that I was probably not the oldest, or the most out of shape, or the weirdest, or the drooliest, or the morning-breathiest person he had to monitor in any given week. I'm sure I'm not the only one that occasionally passes gas in the middle of the night.

Somehow, I fell asleep, despite the fact that I was admonished not to sleep in my favorite position. Prince Charming awoke me with a kiss, ahem, I mean the sleep tech guy woke me by saying my name a few times, and I was told to peel the sensors off of the places I could reach. This was a sticky, gooey, difficult proposition, and for a couple more days, I was still finding them in odd places on my body.

But the good news is that the mask worked, and I was eventually given a CPAP machine of my own to sleep with. I look ridiculous in the mask. It looks more or less like a fighter pilot mask, complete with accordioned tube connecting me to the machine.

CPAP stands for "Continuous Positive Air Pressure." You have a mask that fits either just over your nose, or over your nose and mouth (I have the nose and mouth variety) and it shoots air into your breathing-holes at enough pressure to keep your throat open so that you don't choke on your own flesh like you do when you have sleep apnea. It's kind of fun to play with while you're lying there waiting for sleep to take over.

I always think of this picture I took of my son several years ago, as he was playing with a shop vac:

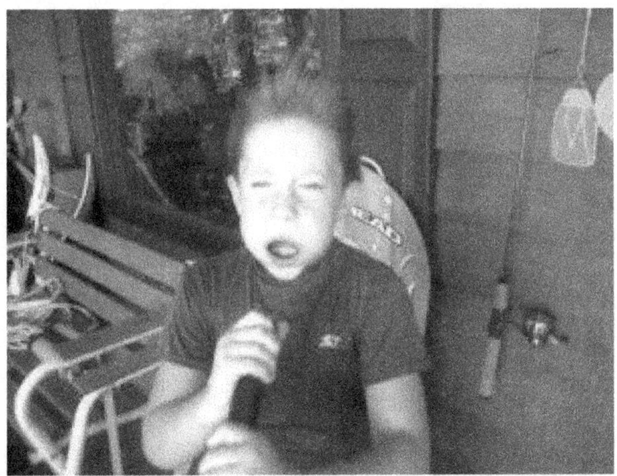

The sleep machine mask looks weird and it took some getting used to, but I have to admit it works. It makes much less noise than you'd think it would, just a quiet and steady "shhhhhhh" like soft rain or a ceiling fan. I get used to the air pressure, and then when I turn it off in the morning I find myself sucking in air for a couple of breaths. I forget how much work it is to have to draw air in under my own power.

I wonder if for some reason I had a heart attack or something in the middle of the night that the machine would count as CPR.

I'm still exhausted all the time, but that's probably more because of my schedule and the teetering piles of stuff loaded on my plate. My brain doesn't feel as fuzzy. I'm more productive. But the best thing of all is that I'm told that I no longer snore. So everyone else sleeps better, too.

Most Likely To ...

It is May and that means it is nearing the end of the school year, which in turn means that there are eighty kabillion dinners, awards ceremonies, and concerts. Each of these has speeches of appreciation which, while sincere, are more or less identical. We couldn't do it without the dedication of... hard work and ... this is the best group of kids who... I'm never going to forget...

And there are awards and certificates and trophies galore. No kid goes home empty handed, even if it's just for the "kindest smile" or "most helpful" award, or for perfect attendance which has always seemed to me to be the award you get when you go to school even when you're sick and infect everyone else.

So I was getting ready to go to my eleventy-twelfth such ceremony of the season, and I was talking to my friend, the hilarious writer Gina Valley, whose website she did NOT pay me to plug, and which can be found here: http://www.ginavalley.com. So Gina suggested that we give awards to the parents instead of the children and we began naming awards.

If you ever want to have a good time, just read over the shoulder of a humor writer who is talking to another humor writer via private Facebook message about something they both think is funny.

Here's a list of awards and superlatives Gina and I think should be given out to the parents at all school related ceremonies. This would increase attendance and definitely increase attention.

- Most Likely to Flirt with the Gym Teacher. (wink wink)
- Best History Project completed entirely by a parent.
- Most Likely to Have a Misspelled Tattoo.
- Most Likely to Get Cat Hair in the Baked Goods.
- Most Obvious Hangover at a Parent-Teacher Conference.
- Most Likely to Throw a Punch at a Ball Game.
- Best Brown-Noser.
- The PTO Mom You Most Avoid Eye-Contact with For Fear She Will Volunteer You For Something.
- Most Likely to Bring Nutter Butters to a Peanut Free Classroom.
- Most Likely to Raid Her Teenage Daughter's Closet.

And for the kids ...

- Most Likely to Steal the Principal's Car.
- Best Piercing Obtained in the Girls' Bathroom.
- Best Eyeroll.
- Most Sarcastic (Gina and I are both fighting over whose kid gets to win this one.)
- Most Likely to Stab a Peer.
- Most Likely to *Be* Stabbed by a Peer.
- Most Likely to Write a Bestselling Tell All Memoir.

And I get why they don't, but I'm convinced that the schools arts programs could be fully funded if they just sold wine at these things, and conscripted teachers to be designated drivers (for tips) afterwards.

Yesaholics Anonymous

Hello. My name is Lori, and I'm a Yesoholic.

I have a more or less clinical resistance to saying no to whatever people ask of me. In fact, even when I say no, people take it as a yes. For example, when I was nominated as the secretary of the middle school band boosters my response was, and I quote, "I respectfully decline the nomination." Five minutes later I was voted in and two years later I'm still the secretary. I think I said no twenty or more times to being the editor for the newsletter for the Georgia Association for Women Lawyers. That didn't work either.

This all came to mind this afternoon when Facebook popped up a memory for me from six years ago today, when I proudly announced that I said "No" to something. It was a big deal then. Apparently it has been six years since I said "No" to anything and it stuck.

I think many people—especially women—and more especially Moms—are guilty of this. We feel responsible for the world, somehow, and are egotistical enough to believe that if we personally don't do what is asked of us, there is not one other human that is up to the task. The world will tilt on its axis and possibly stop spinning altogether.

And so, cribbing from Alcoholics Anonymous, a program which has had huge success in helping people with alcohol addiction, I offer the 12 Steps of Yesaholics Anonymous:

1. We admitted we were powerless over saying yes—that our lives had become an unmanageable tangle of PTO fundraisers, scout meetings, and carpool lines.
2. We came to believe that a Power greater than ourselves (specifically, the word "No") could restore us to sanity.
3. We made a decision to turn our will and our lives over to the care of the suckers who had not yet learned to say "No."
4. We made a searching and fearless moral inventory of our ridiculously inflated egos that make us think we are personally responsible for the success of every stupid little thing that comes along.
5. We admitted to God, ourselves, and to every human being that will stand still long enough to listen the exact nature of our exhaustion borne of saying yes to every little stupid thing.
6. We were entirely ready to have the word "No" remove our defects of character.
7. We humbly say "No" and ask other people to do stuff instead of us. Or leave it undone. Not our problem anymore.
8. We made a list of all persons we had harmed by failing to meet deadlines or doing a half-witted job, and became willing to make amends to them.
9. We made direct amends to such people, such as throwing money at the problem or buying store bought cupcakes, except when to do so would injure them or others. (I'm talking to you, Mom who insists on putting walnuts in the brownies even though we all know good and well there are three allergic kids in the class.)
10. We continued to take personal inventory, and when we were wrong, promptly admitted we were fools for taking this on and delegated it to the next sucker.
11. We sought through prayer and meditation to improve our

conscious contact with the word "no," praying only for knowledge of the healing powers of the word and the power to actually say it out loud when someone asks us to do something.

12. Having had a spiritual awakening as the result of these steps, we tried to carry the message to other Yesaholics, and to practice these principles in all of our affairs.

One day at a time, my friends. It works if you work it. Fake it 'til you make it. It's easy to talk the talk, but you have to walk the walk.

And I am walking the walk, my friends. Out the door, and shouting "No" at the top of my lungs.

The Nine PTO Moms (and One Dad) You See at Every Event

If you've volunteered at any school or PTO event, you know these parents. They're the same in every school across the world. Do you recognize them? More to the point—do you recognize yourself?

1. Marge N. Charge—Marge is seriously bossy. She doesn't care about your agenda. Her agenda is to make this the most successful bake sale in the history of the PTO. This bake sale matters to her. The fate of the free world hangs in the profits. You will do what she says, and you will do it now, with no complaint or variation. You don't like Marge much, but you're glad she's around because it means you don't have to be in charge of anything.
2. Dressy Betsy—Betsy came to this event dressed like she's going out for cocktails. She's wearing impractical heels, lots of jewelry, and she spent at least 45 minutes fixing her hair. Her manicure will get in the way of tying balloons but, God bless her, at least she showed up.
3. Mike (or Doug or Steve) Beige—There's always one lonely, hapless guy. He wants to be a good Dad, and he's trying, but he is totally overwhelmed by the room of women. If there's

a job grilling or carrying stuff, he's on it. He's wearing khaki cargo pants and a polo shirt, and one of his shoes is untied. He makes two or three bad jokes, and then gives up and only speaks when spoken to.

4. BeeBee Stinger—BeeBee is the woman who hasn't stopped moving since her son started Pre-K. She cut seven hundred and fifty stars out of white felt simply because Marge told her to. She doesn't even know what they are for. She is the one who does the icky jobs no one else wants to do. No one asked her to do them, she just did them because they needed to be done. She gets none of the credit. Most people don't even know her real name.
5. Jabba the Mom—Jabba thinks she's Marge, or maybe she thinks she's BeeBee, but she's really just in the way. She is always standing exactly where you need to be. You've never seen her do any actual work, but boy is she tired from not doing it.
6. Mother Mary—Mother Mary wants you to know what she sacrificed to be here to monitor the tug o' war at field day. No one's life is harder, or more difficult, or contains more reasons why she should not be required to volunteer. But she is here, because it is *All About the Children* (clutches chest.)
7. Drama Mama—Drama Mama works alongside you pouring popcorn into little bags at Bingo Night. She seems nice and friendly, but fifteen minutes in you know all about her impending divorce and the reasons therefor. You also know why her brother is in jail, and why child protective services got involved that one time. She might or might not show you a scar. You smile and nod a lot.
8. Bahama Mama—Bahama Mama has a flask in her purse. She will probably let an f-bomb fly a few times. The kids all love her the most.

9. Gladys Kravitz—Gladys knows everydangthing about everydangbody, and she tells you each of those things in a stage whisper that's just a little bit too loud. You have no idea if you are supposed to laugh or be horrified.
10. Last Minute Lisa—Last Minute Lisa has the best of intentions. She pinned the cutest Halloween cupcakes on her aspirational Pinterest board and went so far as to buy two-thirds of the necessary ingredients, including the hard to find black licorice whips. But when push came a-shoving, she showed up twenty minutes late with a box of off brand chocolate chip cookies.

Which one are you? Did I miss one?

P.S. I assume it is painfully obvious that I am Lisa.

The Wednesday of My Life

It's summer, summer being defined as "that period of time in which you don't have to get up and go to school," and that conjures up a lot of images. Long, lazy days in the sun; books to be read; frozen drinks; swimming; and all manner of recreational activities.

Except for us working folks, for whom summer mostly means that it is hot out and I will sweat through my dress clothes even before the hot flashes begin mid-afternoon. I guess there is also less traffic during school hours.

This morning was a typical summer morning in the Duff household. When I left the house at a relatively late 8:30 a.m. (much better than the school year 6:45 a.m.) I was the only vertical member of my family. With two kids and a retired husband sharing my house, no one else need put on pants before noon. Sometimes after that. If at all.

I understand that my husband is older than me, and when he was my age he was still working, so theoretically I don't begrudge him his ability to sleep in as long as he likes. He paid his dues, working thirty years in public safety for DeKalb County.

Intellectually, I know that.

However, when I am slapping the snooze button for the third time, and I see him lying there all peaceful like and making those snuffling noises I used to think were cute, I want to brain him with a shovel. When I leave the house and all three of them are still dreaming tangerine dreams of marmalade skies, I want to clang frying pans together and march up and down the hallway. If I have to get up and face the day, so does everyone else.

But I don't, because I'm a grownup, no matter what my inner whack-job fantasizes about. I do want the people I love to be happy, and they look happy, snug in their beds, the little ... [and here I would insert a bad word which, literally translated, would cast aspersions upon their parentage, and since I am 50% of the parentage of 2/3 of them, I probably ought not.]

Jealousy is an ugly emotion, made uglier when it is irrational. Mine is only partially irrational, as any rational person would be jealous of those with no particular plans for a blue sky summer day when that rational person had to go to work to deal with the intensive drama of other people's lives.

But I was there, then, and I will be there, one day. I don't want to be older, as I have to be before I retire. My odometer is spinning faster and faster these days, which is good, because the spinning wheels create a little breeze which helps cool me down some in these hot days. But pretty soon (it feels like) I won't have any more miles left. I'm not rushing that. And you couldn't pay me to go back to middle school. Or high school for that matter. I don't want to be that girl I was in the '80s, that intense ball of insecurity and uncertainty. It took me decades to be comfortable in my own skin, and now that I am, I don't want to go back to the days where I was my own harshest critic. I've never met anyone who wishes they were 13 again.

So I guess I'll go to work. I'll be thankful I have a job to grumble about getting up for, and be thankful I'm no longer living in the soup of hormones that is middle school and that I (statistically speaking) have so many years of my life left to live.

I'm in the Wednesday of my life. Just like Wednesday afternoon is exhausting because you've already worked enough to be tired but there's so much still to do before the weekend comes; in the middle-aged Wednesday of my life, I'm exhausted because I worked for so many years and there are so many years left to go.

So I'll let my babies sleep in. They need to rest up. Their Wednesday will come.

Time For a Snack Break

I want to say that I'm not obsessed with food. Don't get me wrong—I like food, I like it just fine. It is more than a simple vehicle for nutrients to enter my body. It can be social, pleasurable, and comforting all at once. But I'm not *obsessed.* I don't think about food more than 57 minutes out of every hour. I don't wonder about what I'm going to have for dinner before I'm done with lunch. It's just a pleasurable thing I interact with a few times a day, no different than…than…than…

Okay, I can't think of anything. I do like to eat. Maybe I am obsessed. The number of words I've written on the topic would make you think that.

So, join me. Get yourself a bowl of something salty and crunchy, pour yourself a drink, and let's read about food.

I'm Having a Food Baby

'Tis the season for many things, gluttony being somewhere near the top of the list. Seeing that it's December as I write this, there are a never-ending string of parties and luncheons, boxes of cookies, home-made goodies, and general mass consumption of all things yummy.

I feel like I've spent most of the past three weeks on line at a buffet. Starting with Thanksgiving, followed quickly by a sushi buffet, then a salad bar restaurant, and then the first of many holiday-themed parties. Plus, our yearly foray to Golden Corral after my son's All State Band audition, at which my son and his friend Sydney, between the two of them, ate fifteen or sixteen cones of cotton candy in addition to all the yeast rolls and whatever else they piled on. It was a teenage carb-tastic extravaganza.

I know that if you have a dog, and you are going to be gone for, say, two meal times, you can't leave two meals worth of food out because the dog will eat all the food to the point where the dog will get sick and throw up all over the one square foot of your carpet that is still white, because dogs don't have enough self-control (or sense) to quit eating when they are full. I kinda feel like that these days. The pleasure my mouth gets from the food over-rides the uncomfortable food baby kicking me in the gut.

I don't know why I do this. I know what I'm doing when I do it, and I know I'm going to regret it. But—I mean, we're talking Cherry Cobbler and Banana Pudding. It would be a CRIME to say no or even to choose between them. What kind of an inhumane Sophie's Choice is that?

This is such an American problem. I sat in the Golden Corral last weekend, watching my fellow countrymen and women stack plates upon plates of fried chicken and green beans, marshmallowy sweet potatoes, pasta, pizza, stir fry, non-vegetarian vegetables, carved meats, and you name it into Jenga-like stacks on the table before getting up to get more plates. I wondered if this sort of all-you-can-cram-down-your-gullet emporium even existed in other countries, and I doubted it. I thought about all the people in the world who have to tote unclean drinking water in pots on their heads to their straw homes where they'd eat rice (again) for dinner, and thought about how obscene the whole thing was.

Not so obscene as to prevent me from pouring gravy on my mashed potatoes, mind you, but obscene, nonetheless.

I wasn't sure I could move. I had made the rookie mistake of wearing pants with a definitive waistband complete with constricting button. This made my food baby lodge between my ribs, up where my lungs usually did their thing, so my breathing was labored. I made jokes about the number of paper cotton candy cones piling up on the table, but didn't do much to stop them. I fooled myself into thinking that because one of my plates was entirely covered with salad, and another was entirely covered with vegetables, including but not limited to voluntarily eaten Brussels sprouts and collard greens, that there was a good bit of nutritional value in what I was eating. Which is true, I suppose, but in the same way that there is a good bit of nutritional value in the entire produce section of a grocery store, even though you wouldn't normally eat all of it in one sitting.

I have, at least, learned this much: always scope out the entire buffet before filling your plate. Sometimes the best stuff is at the end, and you don't want your plate to be too full of the stuff that's just OK so that you don't have room for the great stuff.

Last night was the first night of Hanukkah, and I found myself in Athens, GA, home of the University of Georgia, with some friends and a number of our children. We decided to have dinner at the Varsity, an Atlanta area institution, best known for its chili dogs and fried goodies. It seemed fitting to celebrate the first night of the miracle of the oil that lasted for eight days with a greasy, oily dinner that would sit in our collective bellies for the remainder of the eight-day holiday. Another food baby borne of the holiday season.

I think I've got a pretty healthy body image. I mean, I know I'm not thin, but neither am I especially huge. I'm basically healthy, and my body does what I ask it to with minimal complaint. I'm tall-ish, big and strong, and can fit in airplane seats and on carnival rides. I can touch my toes and tie my shoes without my belly getting in the way. But lately I feel like it is a contest to see how much I can stuff in my mouth and still find the strength to haul my carcass up a flight of stairs. I've got to drag me, my clothing, my purse, and twenty-seven pounds of buffet food and onion rings wherever I go. That's no small task.

Nope, there's nothing small about any of this.

But it is delicious.

Grits and Vegemite

I have a friend named Alex, who is the mistress of www.alexchristopherwrites.com and the creator of "Visibility Coaching." Alex lives in Australia, which is about as far from my house in Loganville, GA,as you can get and still be on planet Earth. I met her online, which sounds creepy, but it isn't because it was for business reasons. I'd never met her in person, but I knew what she looked like and sounded like because of the wonders of thc internet.

So, when Michelle Kulp had her Ocean Writing retreat in Annapolis and Alex was going, I figured I had very few excuses about the distance I had to travel, and I went, too. Alex promised to bring Australian food with her. I promised to bring southern food.

Then I had to figure out what transportable southern food was, with a dash of "you probably don't have this in the southern hemisphere." I went to the Stone Mountain Pecan Company for inspiration. I walked out with butter toffee pecans, praline pecans (my favorite), peach butter, and, of course, grits. I found pickled okra elsewhere.

Alex brought two tins of biscuits, these chocolate covered licorice things, "furry friends" chocolates, and chocolate caramels. She also brought Vegemite to make sandwiches with, just like the six-foot-four guy full of muscles in Men at Work's "Down Under."

Those biscuits turned out to be cookies, but, since we called them biscuits, I felt perfectly justified eating them for breakfast.

I made grits. Grits, in case you are reading this from north of the Mason-Dixon Line, are corn. Corn kernels are dried and ground, and then you boil them with water or milk and butter and salt and whatever else you want to put in them to make a kind of porridge. They're better than they sound from that description, and they are a southern breakfast staple. You can also find them at dinner along with shrimp. When I make grits at home, I make them savory. I use bouillon instead of water, I add garlic and sharp cheddar cheese. I like them with a lot of flavor. This time, I made them plain, with just a dash of salt and cream.

Then we set about experimenting. We added Swiss cheese. We sprinkled them with sugar. We added a spoonful of peach butter.

It was all good. Grits are good no matter what you do. They don't have a whole lot of their own flavor, so if you add something yummy, they are going to taste like the yummy thing. Grits are pretty much a vehicle for whatever yummy thing you put on them.

Suddenly, Alex had an inspiration. She held out the little jar of Vegemite. Vegemite, in case you didn't know, is a yeast paste. Australians are sold on the idea that it's good for you because it might have a vitamin in it. It's thick and black and sticky, kind of like used motor oil, only saltier. We took a small spoonful and mixed it with the grits.

And it was good.

Really good.

We think we have a thing here. Australian-American haute fusion cuisine. We want credit, though honestly neither of us has the creative energy to make it happen. That doesn't stop us from wanting our pictures on the packaging. We are the idea people, and we want everyone to sing our praises because of it.

Unless you think it's gross. Then it's all Alex's fault.

Packing Healthy Lunches the Lazy Mom's Way

In 8th grade, my son was assigned to a class called "Family and Consumer Science." This class is, basically, Home Ec, and it irritates me that it is called "Family and Consumer Science" in the way that it irritates me that English class is now called "Language Arts." But that's a 'me' thing, and not at all the point I'm trying to make.

The point is that I am not at all the kind of Mom who is going to buy a Bento Box and artfully arrange in-season fruits and vegetables to look like Disney characters for my kids' lunches. They are lucky if we have a not-expired-for-long Lunchables in the fridge, or if they have money on their lunch accounts. What? You mean I can put $100.00 on their account in the beginning of the year and then not worry about it for a long while? Sign me up.

But then Jacob took Home Ec[22]. Every time any food gets eaten or purchased, we get a lecture about trans-fats. I've only met Ms. Traylor, the Home Ec[23] teacher, maybe once or twice in my life, but I hear her name almost every day. "Ms. Traylor says if you put Ranch on your salad, it's basically like eating dessert." "Ms. Traylor says we have to buy whole

---

22. Sorry. Family and Consumer Sciences. What-freaking-ever.

23. I know. FAMILY AND CONSUMER FREAKING SCIENCES!

wheat flour." Jacob will walk down the junk food aisles in the grocery store shaking his head sadly. "Ms. Traylor got in my head," he admits.

Which isn't a bad thing, necessarily. I am aware of the benefits of good nutrition. I know from experience, for example, that if I go to a street festival and eat a funnel cake and some fried Oreos for lunch, and then go to a questionable Mexican restaurant for dinner, there's going to be fire in my belly for a little while. I try, with varied success, to keep fresh fruit on hand at all times, and to serve a vegetable with every meal. ("Ms. Traylor says that canned vegetables have too much sodium and don't have very many vitamins." Ms. Traylor can come to my house and cook, then, can't she?)

So, with a snippy 14-year-old in my house who insists on reading every label and who is convinced that school lunches are a government plot to make everyone diabetic and obese; and with my abject inability to a) wake up early enough to make him lunch, b) have the wherewithal to make it the night before, or c) keep enough supplies on hand for him to make it himself, we have a real problem.

Plus, I feel bad for the kid. He's 14. He wants to eat loads of crap. He lives in my house—he knows that junk food is comfort food. But every time he tries, he gives himself a guilt trip. So I've looked long and hard for something he can eat that isn't "kale chips, now with extra gag reflex!" Many health foods taste like, well, health food. Also, it can be insanely expensive. Jacob has a mild peanut allergy, and I'm allergic to soy, which makes everything that much more difficult.

Popcorn works, most of the time, but it isn't terribly portable due to the crush factor, and it gets stale in about 23 seconds. I think we finally found our snack food home in Honchos, which are a whole lot like Doritos, only you can pronounce every single one of the ingredients, another one of Ms. Traylor's strict rules. I like the Nacho Cheese, because, well, cheese. (An aside, what exactly is a 'nacho'? Is it an adjective that modifies cheese? Is it a specific flavor? What makes cheese 'nacho' other than being on a chip?) Jacob likes the Peach Habanero, mainly because he likes everything that is slightly off center, and he likes the little warm buzz you get on your tongue about fifteen seconds after you swallow it. And, I can find them at Kroger, another bonus.

I still look in amazement at the lunches on Pinterest, and I wonder if anyone in the history of ever has actually pulled that sort of thing off on a regular basis. I also wonder if the child recipients of those things don't try to trade their cauliflower poodles for a Ding Dong every time they can.

I'm realistic. I'd rather just give him a lunch he'll eat.

How a Cupcake Can Save the World

If you've ever spent more than, say, ten minutes with me, you'll know that one of my greatest fears in life is that someone, somewhere may be the slightest bit hungry. I carry a big Mom-purse that usually has snacks in it. I have indestructible foodstuffs stashed in the glove compartment[24] of my car. In my office conference rooms there are large baskets of junk food. I have a drawer in my desk with canned goods and dehydrated proteins. I keep a jar of peanut butter around at all times. When away from home, one of the most important conversations to have at lunch is what to have for dinner and where we are going to have it.

I wish I could say that I had stashes of high quality food, but while I am prone to exaggeration for effect, I am not a liar. In order to remain what passes for fresh, or at least non-botulism-ed, I tend to have stashes of food with a lot of preservatives in them. If you put fresh strawberries in your purse, you will have fermented strawberry mush in no time at all. Strawberry flavored Starbursts, however, last a while. Likewise, I can't keep grilled chicken breast in my desk drawer or a steak in the pocket of my car door, but I can keep a can of chicken salad with some crackers or beef jerky.

---

24. Seriously—when is the last time that anyone has actually used the glove compartment to store gloves? It's where you put fast food napkins, straws, expired insurance cards, coupons, and a dried out pack of baby wipes.

People make fun of me—a lot—for this (those) habit(s). But those same people eat my food. These are the same people who make fun of me for bringing donut holes to almost every pot luck. But who is the one who doesn't ever bring home leftovers? And why spend time in the kitchen getting the food processor dirty and using fresh ingredients to make a fancy vegetable dip when everyone will just scarf up the one-spoon-and-a-bowl onion-soup-and-sour-cream crapola instead?

Why indeed? I think of myself less as a junk food apologist as someone who is simply more honest than most gourmands. Fancy $3.00-a-piece cookies are great and all, but are they really better than $3.00-a-package Oreos?

Case in point: I gave one of my writing seminars the other day. The kind where we spend all day in a room getting over our fears and ending up with a publishable short story. I know that food and coffee soothe the savage beast, so I spent a ton on snacks. In addition to the junk food basket, I got fresh baked muffins and cookies; fixin's for sandwiches, including fresh peppers, onions, and spinach; coleslaw and potato salad; and bakery bread. My students ate some of that. But I'll tell you what: they all pulled Hostess cupcakes and Twinkies out of the snack basket. "I haven't had one in forever!" They said after long, vaguely R-Rated moans. "Lord, these things are good."

That's some truth telling right there: a roomful of educated, professional women with a high-minded mission will choose snack cakes with a shelf life longer than their own lives over cookies from a bakery. Every single time.

I mean, obviously kale has more nutritional benefits, and you should eat salads and vegetables and lean proteins and whatnot the majority of the time. I'm all for subtle spices and interesting sauces and fig-and-prosciutto flatbreads. But there are times when a Ding Dong or a Ho-Ho can soothe the savage beast like nothing else.

And sometimes, this beast needs soothing.

Overcomplicated Coffee

According to the fancy framed diplomas on my wall, I'm a pretty educated person. I've read a lot of books, written a lot of papers, and researched about a bazillion topics.

None of which prepared me for the coffee maker at my friend's house. My friend, who I've known since the late '80s, graciously allowed my crazy family to stay at her house for 48 hours while we had Things to Do in the town in which she lived. She told us to make ourselves at home. She was a great hostess.

So, when the coffee pot ran dry, rather than ask her to stop what she was doing and make us more coffee, I took it upon myself to brew some more.

It's coffee. I've been making pots of coffee for the better part of forty years. It isn't hard. If you get coffee grounds in contact with hot water, you will have coffee of some sort. That's really all there is to it. I've used all kinds of different coffee makers, drip brews, percolators, cafetieres, French presses, Keurig and Keurig imitations, espresso makers, and, when desperate, a saucepan. None of them tripped me up.

And so, fearlessly and recklessly, I ground the appropriate amount of beans in the grinder from the jar of beans next to the coffee maker, and pulled the carafe out of the machine in order to rinse it out and refill it with clean water. I brought it over to the sink, and twisted the little twisty part on the top. The little twisty part popped off, but there still wasn't a hole in the top of the carafe. There was another little plastic part that was not budging. I pinched. I pulled, I twisted and pressed, grunted and cajoled, and nothing happened. I called my fourteen-year-old son over to see if I was missing the obvious. He couldn't figure out how to open it either.

Eventually, I put the first little plastic part back on, and figured out that you had to push that down while twisting to 'unlock' something or another, and then the whole top came off. Okay then. I washed out the pot and filled it with water, ready for step two.

I went to pull out the basket where the coffee grounds went. The coffee maker, a slick looking shiny chrome model, had the basket in the regular place, but the drawer thingie that it sat in was aesthetically flush with the rest of the machine. This made it look very modern and hip, but no amount of my sticking my thumbnail between the cracks would make it pop out. I called my son over again. Eventually, he found a little chrome button on the side which shot it forwards with surprising force.

The grounds put into place, the only thing left was to pour the water in the top. I pulled on the top of the coffee maker, and the plastic piece on top came out, revealing a round plastic piece, which also pulled off. There was something that looked like a drain at the bottom, so I poured the water in it. And, in so doing, poured water all over my foot, the floor, and the cabinet. This was not where the water went, or, maybe it was, only I didn't do the magic incantation that allowed its essence to flow into the part where it came in contact with the magic beans. We could not figure out how to make it stop. Finally, my daughter, with all 12 years of wisdom behind her, thought to put a cup underneath it to catch the water. Duh.

A roll of paper towels later, we got the mess cleaned up, but then couldn't figure out how to get the round part back on the top. As I stood there with a confused look on my face, my friend emerged from her shower, looking clean and well-scrubbed and ready to face the day and the morons in her kitchen who couldn't operate the coffee maker.

I'm not sure if this is a commentary on the over-complication of a simple job, or pointing out how useless a dean's list certificate from a major university is when facing the tasks of daily living that actually matter. Or maybe it is just an ode to my old Corningware percolator with the three blue flowers on the side that anyone who could light a stove could operate because there aren't any other options.

If you need me, I'll be pondering this philosophical question at a coffee shop, where someone else can worry about where the water goes.

Jackfruit

My son and I have a rule, which is that every time we go to a grocery store, we pick some kind of food we've never had before and we buy it. He always tries it. I only try it 85% of the time. For example, I did not try the tinned octopus. We've found some good stuff this way (lychee nuts), and we've also found some stuff we can't believe anyone voluntarily puts into their mouths (this nasty Jamaican drink that was chunky and foamy and might just have been regurgitated.)

My daughter, whose diet consists mainly of mac 'n' cheese, chicken nuggets, and French fries, with the occasional nod towards apple slices and Swedish fish, rarely participates. However, one day not too long ago Marin and I were in the grocery store picking up specific ingredients for something or another, when a weird looking thing in the produce department stopped us in our tracks.

"What is that?" my daughter said.

I didn't know. It could be a dragon egg, or maybe a spaceship. It was huge, maybe the size of the biggest watermelon you've ever seen, but more irregularly shaped, and it was bumpy. It was a mottled yellow/brown/green color. Marin reached out her hand to touch it and immediately drew it back. "It hurts!"

I looked at the label. It was a "Jackfruit." I had never heard of such a thing. It was only 99 cents a pound. We tried to pick it up to get a better idea of it, but it was difficult. You had to hold it just so or the bumps on it dug into your hand. It was heavy. It required as much forearm as hand for lifting. We managed to get it up and out and over to the produce scale without dropping it or drawing blood. The thing weighed 21 pounds. So, even though it was only 99 cents a pound—which is cheap for apples—it would still cost over 20 bucks. For an unknown.

Marin developed an unnatural attachment to it.

The produce guy wandered by and asked us if we needed help. We asked him about the jackfruit, and he said it tasted like a sweet melon, kind of like a cross between a cantaloupe and a banana. He said it was very good.

In a weak moment, and mostly because I knew I'd get a chapter out of it and therefore could deduct the expense on my taxes, I bought it. We buckled it in the back seat to get it home, what with it being as large as a four-year-old.

When we got home, we searched on YouTube to figure out what we were supposed to do with it. We learned that if it isn't ripe then the core and the rind can leak latex which will get all over your knife and your cutting board and your hands. So you should wear gloves and oil your knife and cover your cutting board. Then you carve the thing in two halves. Inside are these yellowish soft pods. Each pod has a seed in it which is hard and kind of a pretty swirly brown. I learned you should save the seeds, and cook and eat them like chestnuts.

You have to dig your hand into the jackfruit to get the pods out, and then strip it of this fibrous material that, if you had the patience, you could probably weave into a pretty strong rope. You pop the seed out and eat the flesh. It took us nearly an hour to make the carnage you see in that picture.

It was good. A mild melony flavor, almost like eating flowers. And not anywhere near worth the colossal effort. It took my son and I[25] about an hour before we gave up, and we got about a gallon of fruit and a quart of seeds out of it.

My kitchen was a disaster. It took two days to get all the latex off the knife and I'm still finding little pieces of fiber on the kitchen floor.

There's only so much jackfruit you can eat, so I looked up what you could do with it. I'm told you can cook it like pork—barbecue it or jerk it—and pretend like it is BBQ. You can also cook it into a curry. We haven't tried this yet. It remains in a plastic bag in our fridge, daring me to try something culinary with it.

Maybe I will, and maybe I won't. I don't have to tell you jack. Jackfruit, that is.

---

25. My daughter gave up after about five minutes. I successfully resisted the urge to pelt her with jackfruit seeds for her lack of dedication to her own cause.

Sometimes You Do What I Ask

Those moments, fewer and further between than I'd like them to be, where everything goes the way it should are the moments I live for. The people in my life, my family and my friends and co-workers, are good people. If they weren't good people, they wouldn't be in my life. True, I complain a lot about what they do (and don't do.) But I do it for the same reason that some teachers are harder on the good students than they are on the ones with little promise. I'm not going to spend my time on you if you aren't going to get anything out of my effort.

So, family and friends and co-workers, consider the fact that I give you grief and complain a compliment. If I didn't care, I wouldn't bother. And thank you for all that you do, including, but not limited to, putting up with me.

Mascara

If I were a little kid, and I presented you with this picture I had drawn with crayons:

you would have no real way of knowing if it was supposed to be a boy or a girl. It's kind of a generic person face. Nothing especially feminine or masculine about it.

However, if I were to present you with this picture:

you would not hesitate to identify it as a female face. If a girl gave you this picture and told you it was a picture of her daddy you would wonder if her daddy perhaps had a career in show business. It's the exact same picture, the only difference is the eyelashes.

Somehow we've decided as a society that of all the things that mark the difference between men and women's faces—the jaw line, the presence of facial hair (though, to be honest, the older I get the less you can tell the difference in that regard between my husband and me,) or even hairstyle, it is the eyelashes that make the difference. This, perhaps, explains the presence of such robust false eyelashes on drag queens—it's like an exclamation point on the "I'm a girl!" message.

And so I found myself one evening in the makeup aisle of Wal-Mart presented with a choice of approximately sixty bajillion different kinds of mascara. I needed mascara. I said that phrase to myself after I selected other items I'd gone to the store for: "I need mascara." Because heaven forbid I should show up at work with pale, short-looking eyelashes with no definition. Someone might think I'm a man[26].

I'm not really a makeup girl. My guess is that once I retire (please buy

---

26. Not that there's anything wrong with that.

my books so I can retire sooner rather than later[27]) I will own one dried out tube of lipstick and some ancient eyeshadow that I will drag out four times a year when I get forced out of the house to go to weddings. But now I work, and makeup is part of the uniform, so it was off to the cosmetics aisle at a discount store for me.

My 12-year-old daughter was with me. Marin is a makeup girl, despite the fact that she rarely wears it. She rarely wears it because (and I think she'll agree with me here) she is inherently lazy and it is a lot of work. Plus, she has a tendency to get out of bed about three minutes before the bus comes, so she has to pare down her routine to nothing but essentials. But she watches a lot of makeup tutorials on YouTube and every once in a while, when she gets a burst of energy, she busts out her "contour palette" and whatever else is in that giant pink case that takes up half the bathroom counter, and comes out looking sophisticated and elegant and twice her actual age. (She is young enough that twice her actual age is still a compliment. Twice my personal age is usually accompanied by the phrase, "And she can still get around pretty well, bless her ancient heart.")

I stood there, stupefied by the range of choices. What in the heck is the actual difference between volumizing and plumping? Why is one three dollars and the other seventeen? All I knew is that I didn't want something that would drip down my face every time my tear ducts activated with a yawn (every twenty seconds in the afternoon.) I noticed another woman, approximately my age, standing there with the same dumb stare on her face.

Eventually my daughter took pity on me. "This is the one you want," she said, pointing to a yellow package.

"Is that the one I want?" I asked, "Or is that the one you want to swipe out of my drawer to use yourself?"

---

27. #ShamelessSelfPromotion

"Both," she said.

Then I noticed. There were two different yellow packages, one with one stripe, one with two. "What's the difference?" I asked.

After a middle-school worthy eye-roll she said, "One has a curved brush, and one has a straight brush." She said this like it would be useful information for me; like it would explain something.

I waited for further explanation, but none came. So I prompted, "And?"

She made a noise that might have been made by a predatory cat. She grabbed a package off the wall and threw it in the cart.

I saw the other woman grab the same package and throw it in her own cart. "Thank you," she mouthed at me. I nodded sagely.

We all have to share our daughters when it helps. Especially the ones that watch YouTube.

Grilled Cheese and Snuggles

The other day, my daughter was sad for reasons only truly understood by another 12-year-old girl. It was a Saturday, one of the few days in which I had nothing in particular to do, and to celebrate planned on doing laundry and scrubbing the grout in the bathroom.

Marin moaned something pitiful and fierce, and handed me a frying pan. "I want grilled cheeeeeeeeeeeeeeeeeeeeeese."

I raised my eyebrows in a way that I hoped communicated the fact that she was plenty old enough to make her own grilled cheese and I had my own things to do.

Then she did the puppy dog eyes. Looking up through her lashes, she said, "And tomato soup. It tastes better when you make it."

I sighed a put-upon sigh and got to making the soup and sandwich.

Between dramatic noises, I gathered that the sadness came from her sudden realization that she was two-thirds of the way through childhood. Adulthood and all its attendant responsibilities were hurtling towards her on a collision path, like a drunk driving on the wrong side of the Interstate.

I stuck *Ratatouille* in the DVD player, the first DVD I found in our collection that was both childlike and didn't make me want to throw up. We sat together on the sofa, eating our grilled cheese and tomato soup, and then snuggling in to watch the movie. From somewhere a blanket appeared, and we huddled together under it, her head resting against my side and her fingers absent-mindedly playing with the hem of my sleeve.

When was the last time she did this? It had to be years before.

As we watched the movie, my mind wandered, and I started thinking about all the things I needed to get done. The dishes, the loads of laundry, the bills to be paid. I didn't have time to sit on the sofa and do nothing. I started to feel the low level anxiety that is the background noise of my life: the constant pressure to always be moving forward, to meet responsibilities and get it all done before more piles up.

Marin announced her feet were cold, and she tucked them under my thigh for warmth. There was no way I was ever going to move now. My anxiety kicked up a notch, and my bladder reminded me of its capacity. What should I do? I may never be home three hours in a row again to wash and dry and fold a load of laundry all in one shot. I was down to the underwear I'd be embarrassed to be in a car wreck wearing. I was sporting a 15-year-old nursing bra.

But I did nothing. I sat there, enjoying the company of the daughter who spends most of her days pulling as far away from me as she can, as is absolutely normal for a 12-year-old girl. I reached out to see if she would let me stroke her hair, and she did, just like when she was three and we'd watch Tom and Jerry Cartoons on the sofa together. I was painfully aware that this might likely be the very last time we ever did anything like this together, and I did my best to record every single second in my memory banks. I wasn't going to let it slide by, even if it did mean that I had no clean clothes and a filthy kitchen.

Sometimes, doing nothing but eating grilled cheese is important. Sometimes doing nothing is the biggest kind of something you can do.

My Baby Boy is Sick

My sweet little baby boy is sick. He went to school on Tuesday, and almost immediately called to come home from the nurse's office. He had a fever of 100.7, which is a number better seen on a radio dial than a thermometer. Four days later his fever is still there, persistent and visible. We took him to the doctor. He has both the flu and an ear infection.

When he was a baby boy, he had a similar illness and called it an "ear confection," which made me think of his ear filled with some kind of waxy nougat.

I call him my baby boy still, but he isn't really. He's smack in the center of his teenage years, and he's tall enough to put his chin on the top of my head when we're standing next to each other.

He's pitiful this week. His eyes are glassy and his cheeks are flushed and he has no appetite, which is frightening for a boy who regularly eats a dozen eggs at one sitting. I want to pull him up on my lap and stroke his hair and rock him. He didn't even want me to stay home with him. "Mom," he said. "I'm just going to sleep all day. I'm 15. I can make myself tea if I really want it."

Well, yes, he can. He can administer his own Motrin every few hours. He can take his own temperature, and he can heat up frozen chicken soup just as easily as I can. My baby boy is sick, and I just don't know what to do about it.

I'm still his Mommy, and I want to Mommy him.

My Mommymometer still works. I can kiss his forehead and know within a tenth of a degree what his fever is. My husband, who was a paramedic back when the recommended treatment was a good bleeding to get rid of ill-humours, thinks he's the medical expert in the family, but he is horrible at knowing what a sick person needs. And whether that sick person still has a fever.

I do truly get tired of being right all the time.

I go in my son's room from time to time. If he's awake he'll lean his head against my shoulder, or maybe I'll rub his back. I can't wrap his whole fever-warm body up in my arms any more, but I can still love him just as much and push the sweaty bangs away from his face. I can listen to him moan in his newly minted baritone voice about being tired of feeling cruddy. I can stroke the patches of real-and-for-true stubble on his cheek when he tries to sleep it off.

I love him. It breaks my heart that loving him this much isn't enough to cure what ails him.

I'll tell you this much, though. If he gets me sick, he'll be in big trouble. I do love the boy, but even I have my limits. I want to love him, but I do NOT want his germs.

The Bat Mitzvah Girl, the Ogre, and the Onion

Note: On January 14, 2017, my daughter became a Bat Mitzvah. It is traditional for the mother (me) to give a speech going on and on about how awesome her child is. There were so many ways that my daughter was awesome, I didn't know how to list them all without being boring. Then it dawned on me: Shrek. Here's the transcript of my speech.

In the movie *Shrek*, when Shrek and Donkey are getting to know each other, Shrek says, "There's a lot more to ogres than people think. Ogres are like onions."

Donkey says, "They stink? They make you cry?"

Shrek says, "No! Layers! Onions have layers. Ogres have layers. They both have layers!"

Donkey thinks about this and says, "You know, not everyone likes onions. Everyone likes cakes. Cakes have layers."

Shrek, very frustrated, says, "I don't care what everyone likes! Ogres are not like cakes! Ogres are like onions!"

And so, Marin doesn't much care what everyone likes, and she is like an onion. Let us peel back her layers and see what's inside.

On the outside, we see this: a girl of surpassing beauty, with long, heartbreaking legs and luminous blue eyes.

But let's peel that superficial layer away; that's the paper layer that might get your attention, but it isn't going to season your stew. Underneath, you find talent. You've heard today how well she can sing. You may or may not know that she also plays the guitar. She also plays the flute impressively well. Her ear is near perfect—she can hear slight variations in pitch that professional musicians only dream of being able to do. Yes, she's talented all right.

But there's another layer beneath that. Anyone who has talked to her for more than thirty seconds knows how intelligent she is. How she absorbs information instantly and processes it in ways most of us are not capable of. How, when she's paying attention, nothing gets by her. Yes, she's gifted in the true sense of the word.

Yup, beauty, talent, and brains—that would be enough. But there are more layers. Underneath all that is her humor. Ever since she learned to speak she's had an uncanny sense of humor far beyond her years. Her first made up joke, is this one, made before she could even pronounce the words properly: She said to her father, "What's that?"

"What's what?" he responded.

"Your pwobwem." Hilarity ensued. Her Marinisms, her Marin's Quotes of the Day on Facebook have a small cult following. This girl is hilarious.

You think I'm done? Oh heck no. I'm just getting started with layers. Her Achilles heel has always been her empathy. She feels deeply for anyone in pain. She's known as the "mom" of her friend group because she always wants to take care of those around her. She wants everyone to be well, physically and mentally. When I'm sick, she always makes sure I have a teddy bear to cuddle.

This extends to people she doesn't even know. She makes a point of finding something to compliment in every cashier she encounters. It might be their hair, or their eyeliner, or their manicure, or the color of their shirt. She will find something. She will chase people down in stores to give compliments. These random acts of kindness make my heart swell with pride.

You want another layer? Here's another layer—if she wants to, she can and she will. The trick is getting her to want to. But when she does, there is nothing that will stop her.

How about this layer? She is a powerful and loyal friend. When her friends are put on the defensive, Marin is right there defending them as if she were the one offended. Crossing one of Marin's friends is the same as crossing Marin, or maybe the same as crossing a Mama Bear with newborn cubs. She will level you with that death stare that cuts like a light saber. You cannot win an argument against Marin. Trust me—I'm a lawyer, and I've tried. I lose every time.

I'm convinced she will take over the world one day. I'm convinced she will use these powers for good—or at least I hope she will. She's not a cake. Everyone likes cake, but she's not a cake. And here's the thing—you can get sick from too much cake. You can get tired of cake. But not onions. They're versatile and delicious. Marin is an onion, all right. A savory, spicy, sweet, and flavorful onion.

And I love onions. Better than cake.

High School Dance

I'm pretty sure that I only went to one high school dance the entire time I was in high school, and that was the senior prom. It wasn't really called the senior prom, because there wasn't any other prom. It was THE prom. It was a Big Deal. I vaguely remember some other dances existing, but never considered going, nor did any of my friends. I don't know if I was just anti-social or if they just weren't a *thing* the way they are now. I just know I didn't go, which put all the pressure for creating memories on one day in June in 1988.

But here we are, in 2016, and my son, my once-little six and a half pound peanut, is a high school freshman, and there are dances and shindigs every thirty-five seconds, or so it seems. The high school dance culture is a real cottage industry. A money-maker, for sure. There are shops dedicated to selling $300.00 sparkly dresses to 15-year-olds, and other shops dedicated to reselling the gently worn dresses (read: worn once, but not cleaned, because the beads and mirrors and sparkles can't be) for a third of the price. You can't get a haircut or your nails done on a Saturday in October and April here in the deep south, because all the slots are booked in advance by teenagers needing fancier up-dos and nails than I had at my wedding.

The Friday before the homecoming dance is the homecoming football game. I go to all the football games to watch my son march in the band. On homecoming Friday, during halftime, the homecoming court has a grand processional on the field, each evening-gowned girl escorted by her father or her uncle or some other older-dude-of-significance. Stunningly, none of them fall when their four inch heels sink into the football field. Then the homecoming queen from last year crowns the homecoming queen from this year, and the girls are let loose in the stands when the football game continues.

It is kind of entertaining watching these girls in their impractical clothing navigate the bleachers. At least for me, as I was wearing jeans and sneakers and a sweatshirt, it was. Poor babies had to be cold with their shoulders and flat bellies and backs exposed like that. "Here, honey," I wanted to say. "Here's a sweater and a sandwich. You'll catch your death!"

Boys definitely have it easier in this regard, even boys like my son who actually care what they look like. I took the opportunity for a teachable moment to show Jacob how to iron pants and a shirt. He put on his freshly pressed khakis, a white button down shirt he stole from his father, a bow tie, clip on suspenders, and a pair of flat, foot-shaped dress shoes. He combed his hair, brushed his teeth, and he was good to go.

We went to a local park-slash-botanical-garden to take pre-homecoming pictures with the group of friends Jacob was going with. The parking lot was so packed that there were cops there working security. Obviously we were not the only ones there to take pictures. The gardens were littered with uncomfortable looking boys and made-up girls. The girls were pretending like walking along garden paths wearing platform shoes and stilettos was something they could just do, trying hard (and sometimes but not always succeeding) to avoid getting their heels caught in the seams of the wooden walkways. There was a host of dumpy looking parents with cameras trying to get their kids not to smile like *that* or to quit dabbing or doing other stupid dance moves while we preserved the moment for all of history.

One mom asked me if I wanted a picture of me with my son. I looked at him, all polished and handsome, and touched the bandana on my hair, feeling the grease on my un-makeup-ed face and politely declined. I felt like a slug in a butterfly garden. There were too many beautiful, hopeful young people about for me to want to preserve my potato face amongst them.

Which is dumb. Because I know my son loves me, whether or not I am objectively beautiful. And I love him. I'm proud of him, and I'm proud to be his mother. I'm 31 years older than him, which means, statistically, that the last 31 years of his life are likely to be spent with me only as a memory. It's really not fair to make him conjure up my face when I can look at tons of pictures of him.

The truth is that love makes anyone beautiful. Love is the primary source of beauty. And we can all use a little more of that in our lives.

Baby's First Drive-Through

My son turned 15 recently and, in this neck of the woods, that means he got his Learner's Permit. That's right. My bitty baby, born two and a half weeks early, smaller by every measurement than my housecat, is now legally allowed to have primary control of a one ton[28] projectile moving at great speed.

Naturally, I'm a little nervous.

He's generally a cautious kid, but I was not taking any chances. I made him sit through the Traffic Violators Impact Panel, which is kind of a scared straight program for young drivers. After listening to speakers who killed people with cars, hearing from the parents of dead kids, and watching disturbingly graphic and realistic videos, I thought maybe he'd learned something. So I asked him. "Did you learn anything?"

"Yes," he said. "I learned I'm scared to drive."

Mission accomplished.

So here we are. I'd let him drive around deserted parking lots and up our driveway, but never on the real road. It had to happen sometime. It happened last week.

---

28. I actually looked this up. I drive a Honda Accord. The interwebs don't agree on how much a 2010 Honda Accord weighs, but it is anywhere from 2,000 to 3,200 pounds, or more, depending upon a) how many Duffs are in the car; b) whether or not the gas light is on; and c) how long it has been since I cleaned out the trunk.

We were in the car together, and he was whining. Not whining. Asking politely in a very insistent, relentless, manly way. He wore me down.

I pulled into the shopping center near our home and parked. "Take us through Taco Bell," I said, and got out of the car. He hopped in the driver's seat, buckled his seat belt (good boy), and we were off.

He managed to get us through the drive-through lane without scraping the sides of the car. This is something I only accomplish nine out of ten times I go through a drive-through, so I figured we'd call it a success. We both realized at the same time that this would be the first time he would be in charge of talking through the speaker. He choked a little bit, but eventually ordered my 7-layer Burrito like a pro. I took a picture and posted it on Facebook. It was as much a milestone and therefore worth capturing as his first tooth and his first step.

Tacos in hand, it was time to go home. I questioned the wisdom of letting him drive on an actual road. Oh well, I thought. Nothing ventured, nothing gained, and it had to happen eventually.

He did well, if slow. He stayed in his lane.[29] He used his turn signal appropriately. And drove approximately 20 miles under the 55 mile per hour speed limit. He was so slow that the car behind us lost patience and passed us on a double yellow.

There was no objective reason for me to be scared, but I was. Not scared. Nervous. Everything in me was clenched. If I'd had a fistful of charcoal, at the end of the three mile drive I would have had a fistful of diamonds. My muscles were so engaged that lactic acid started to build-up and I wondered if maybe I could consider this an isometric workout. My voice came out as a strangled screech every time I tried to say something.

Eventually we made it home, intact if not efficiently. When he began the climb up our driveway, something he's done a million times before, I unclenched and began to breathe again. In the end, I was proud of him. He conquered his fear, did something new and scary, and didn't kill anyone while he was at it.

That's what I call a good Tuesday.

---

29. Something, according to my 13-year-old daughter, [illegible] incapable of doing.

Get a Job, Kid

"Get a Job, Kid!"

I can't count the number of times I've said this in response to a sentence that starts "Mooooomm! I waaaaant..." Well, my boy finally took my advice.

My boy, who is now so old that if he goes a few days without shaving you can see the stubble on his jawline from ten paces, has needs. Needs I'm not willing to pay for. Needs like vinyl records for his faux-vintage record player. Needs like probiotic drinks in fancy glass bottles that cost, per ounce, more than sterling silver. Needs like the upgraded account to Hulu so he doesn't have to watch commercials during episodes of incomprehensible Anime.

So, approximately 12 years after I first responded "get a job" to his request for something or another, he actually got a job. This is his first work day. He's working from 4-9pm, standing on the side of the road wearing an Uncle Sam costume and twirling a sign. He was hired to be a "sign twirler." We have since dubbed him a "human positional advertisement."

He was excited to get the job. He felt like a responsible person, taking control over his life and feeling the pride of working for what you have. He counted the money he'd make ($7.25 x 5 is $36.50, so after taxes, that's probably $30.00 which means I could buy…) and couldn't wait until it was time to twirl.

So he showed up at the appointed time, an eager, enthusiastic first time employee. He changed into his costume and went to work.

He's disgruntled already, and it is only 6:30.

To be fair, this is the coldest it has been for a while, and there are only so many layers you can fit beneath the costume. It is boring as all get out, standing there for hours on end trying to look cheery while people give you pitying looks from inside their warm cars. It isn't intellectually taxing work. The only skill you need is the ability to stand upright and not accidentally dart into traffic just to end the tedium. Still, it is honest work, it is productive work, and I am hopeful that it will renew his desire to stay in school as long as humanly possible.

I brought him some hot coffee, not so much because I was responding to his pitiful, whining text messages, but more because I wanted to see him and revel in the fact that, for the first time in over 15 years, I was at rest and he was working. Ha. Ha-freaking-ha.

There is a sandwich shop within walking distance of his designated twirling spot, and he begged for a sandwich. Given that it was dinner time, and that one of my primary roles as his parent is to see that he is fed often enough to keep Child Protective Services at bay, I walked over and got a sandwich. I paid $7 and change for a foot long sandwich with no drink or chips. It occurred to me that it would take him more than an hour of standing on the side of the road in 45 degree weather if he were to pay for it himself. I told him this when I gave it to him.

He stood stock still for a moment, absorbing that information. "That's sad," he said. "That's really sad." He thought some more. "How do people…?" He didn't finish his question.

I didn't have much of an answer, because I have no idea how people do. I thank my maker every day that I don't have to know.

I guess my son thought I'd stay and keep him company some, judging from the disappointed look on his face as I got into my late model sedan with the heated seats to go home and do nothing productive for a few hours. But I've paid my dues and I have no interest in overpaying. I worked at Burger King for a few weeks as a teenager. It was a horrible job, smelly and greasy and exhausting. I hated every second of it. I also worked as a cashier in a busy bakery, standing on my feet for eight hours at a time while rude customers barked orders at me. I took to wearing a cap that said, "please say please," which had exactly zero effect on anyone except to cheese off my manager.

Every teenager should have a service job. It makes you a better customer and a better person. You can't start out at the top, and some people never get there. If you haven't spent time in the trenches, how can you know what it's like in a trench?

So I'm glad my Buddy's in a trench, as uncomfortable as it may be. I feel sorry for him, but I'm happy for the education he's getting. And I have a feeling he's going to like that thirty dollars. Probably enough to do it again.

Music Lessons

When I was but a wee babe, the *Partridge Family* was a hit show. I loved it for many reasons, not the least of which was the existence of "Lori Partridge," who justified my name as a cool-girl name. I still hold a grudge against the Romper Room lady for never saying she saw "Lori" when she looked through her magic mirror at her friends at home.

The Partridges were good looking and talented, sure, but they got along reasonably well, and they made music together. My family wasn't musical: I grew up in a family of jocks. My dad played football and my mother was a cheerleader, and they were both natural athletes. This did not pass along to me. I'm lucky to walk across a carpeted room without falling. I can neither run, throw, nor catch. But I am musical.

Playing music with other people has always been my favorite form of communication. Recently, a friend of mine was battling with her ten-year-old son about practicing piano, and she asked the hive mind that is Facebook how to articulate why she thought it was so important that he learn to play the piano. This got me to thinking. Why is music education so important? I mean, sure I could look it up. Goodness knows there are countless articles written on the subject and actual scientific sounding studies done. But that would be work, and I'd rather just tell you what I think.

Music is another language. If you take music lessons and can read music fluently (without stopping to count the lines or spaces and saying to yourself "Every Good Boy Does Fine") you can read another language. You know words in Italian and German. If you learn the piano, you learn to read both treble clef and bass clef—two different alphabets—at the same time! I mean, imagine if you had English instructions for your right hand on the top line, and French instructions for your left hand on the bottom line. Do you think there would be a chance you could follow all those rapid-fire instructions without messing up? That's what piano players do, essentially. Now *tell* me that won't train your brain for complex tasks.

Playing any instrument with any kind of skill forces you to listen intently. If you play a note in a way that makes the number of sound waves per second off by only one or two, there are whole categories of people that will want to rip your ears off. People have very strong opinions about sound waves, about whether a concert "A" should be 440 Hz or 442, or (gasp) 432. Only a trained ear can hear the difference. Tell me that doesn't train you to listen to the nuances in speech.

Music is also about communication. Whenever you play with another person, you have to sense speed, intonation, pull and push, emphasis and unimportance. You have to learn to take a back seat to the melody. You learn that it isn't always your turn, and how a good bass line is like a strong spine. It's in the back, all covered up, and most people aren't even aware of yours. But without it, you'd collapse.

Nothing makes me happier than the fact that my children have turned out to be musical. Occasionally, the planets align, and we are all home with nothing else pressing, and we play trios, my daughter and I on the flute, and my son on the oboe. Sometimes I'll accompany them on the piano. Those are the happiest moments of my life. I mean, we're not the Partridge Family, but we are Grammy worthy, no? Come On! Get Happy! And this from two kids who can't go more than two minutes without calling each other inappropriate names, and who both think I'm the most embarrassing, uncool human on the planet.[30]

I recently accompanied my son during his audition for a music scholarship. He didn't win the scholarship, but he won life, as far as I'm concerned. He dropped his music halfway through, and picked it up on a rest without missing a beat. Yup, that's my kid. In playing piano for him, I got to spend time with him, and we learned lots about how to read each other's non-verbal cues. Plus, since he was the soloist and I was the mere accompanist, he got to be in charge of me. He worked hard, and something beautiful came out at the other end.

I would imagine that teammates playing basketball together would learn many of the same lessons. It doesn't matter how you learn them, so long as they get learned.

And that, my friends, is music to my ears.

---

30. They're not wrong.

Way Back in the Way Back

Back before the laws of physics were passed and no one wore seat belts because we all believed it would be safer to be 'flung free,' my parents owned a big blue Chevy Caprice Station Wagon. My sister and I would fight over who got to sit in the 'way back' amongst the groceries and spare jackets. The way back was desirable because we were small enough to pretend it was necessary to roll around every time the car took a turn or came to a stop.

The Station Wagon wasn't always a mobile amusement park. It was also a war zone, in which the seams on the seat formed the boundaries of demilitarized zones between siblings. The borders were always being pushed by wayward fingers and knees which would result in an escalation of hostilities.

I also remember late nights, which probably weren't all that late, just dark, coming home from wherever and being sleepy. I would stretch out across the big sofa of a back seat and fall asleep. Because I was little. And I could. It didn't occur to me that anything would or could happen but that my parents would wake me when I got home so that I could stumble into my bed. I remember being rolled a little when we came to a hard stop or made a tight turn, but nothing as violent as the head over heels tumble in the way back and it was all just part of the ride. It was like being rocked in a cradle. My dad would have white noise sports talk radio on, or maybe a baseball game on a scratchy AM station[31]. Occasionally my parents would chatter in a stream of mumbles that I paid exactly no attention to. They were there. They were in control. All was right with the world.

Of course, now I strap my kids in like astronauts in 27 point harnesses which will protect them not only from getting a minor boo-boo in a wreck but the powerful force of the side curtain air bags. They are, objectively, safer, but I doubt they feel that way. I think they just feel restrained. Sometimes I catch them lying across the seat trying to take a nap. I yell at them, citing made up exaggerated statistics about how they will become a projectile if I so much as stop at a stop sign, crashing through the windshield after using their thick skulls like battering rams to knock the rest of the passengers unconscious before their exit.

Sometimes ignorance really is bliss.

Over Thanksgiving, I took my little family to visit my parents. On more than one occasion I found myself in the backseat of my parents' car as my dad ferried me and my children to whatever restaurant my mother had a good coupon for[32]. I sat there, relieved not to have to be driving for a change, and stared out of the window while discussing what we were going to do after dinner.

We pulled into the parking lot of the restaurant one night, and it suddenly occurred to me that I had no idea where I was, and if you asked me to drive back to my parents' house without the aid of a GPS I could not. I pride myself on my sense of direction and generally knowing where I stand in relation to the rest of the globe at any given moment. But I had no idea. And I didn't need to know. Because I was blissfully

31. Now, four decades into the future, with the advent of Satellite Radio and CD players, if you get in my Dad's car the radio will still only be tuned to sports talk radio, or maybe a baseball game.

32. We are not allowed to eat in restaurants if my mother doesn't have a coupon.

able to be a little girl, sitting in the back seat of my daddy's car, trusting that someone bigger and more competent than me had it all handled.

On the way home, I wonder if he'll let me sit in the Way Back and roll around at stop signs.

Acknowledgements

Thank you to everyone who has ever said anything nice to me. Thank you to everyone who laughs at my jokes, even when they are only marginally funny or not funny at all. A hearty thank you to everyone who has shelled out a few bucks to buy my books. Y'all are my enablers.

Thank you to Diane Hale, my Southern Baptist Conscience, something every Jewish girl living in the South needs. She unwaveringly knows when I've gotten off base with my writing. Thank you to the Erma Tribe for being the Erma Tribe, and if you were in the Erma Tribe, you'd know what that meant. Potowatomi Princesses—write on with your royal selves. Thank you to the National Society for Newspaper Columnists for mentioning me honorably, and thus giving me some credibility in my own head when I really needed it. Thank you to the Walton Writers' Guild for unwavering love and support and cups of off-brand wine.

Thank you to the Jew Crew for being the Jew Crew and letting me say whatever the eff I want whenever I feel like it without judgment. The Goddesses shall gather!

Thank you to the crew at Deeds Publishing for making everything happen like magic while I went about my business, and for Linda Hughes for her keen editorial eye and suggestions. Y'all should go buy her books to thank her for me.

And, of course, a giant thank you to my family for giving me forgiveness when I write about them without asking for permission first. Also for the hundred ways in which I love them and they support me and make me laugh. I love you guys THE MOST.

CPSIA information can be obtained
at www.ICGtesting.com
Printed in the USA
BVHW031451131220
595622BV00009B/187